A Guide To Crocheting Cute Animals

Emma L. Adams

Introduction

This book is a delightful collection of easy-to-follow patterns for creating adorable crocheted animals. This book is designed for beginners who want to explore the world of amigurumi and crochet their own cute animal companions.

The patterns are divided into three levels to cater to different skill levels. Level 1 patterns are perfect for beginners and introduce basic techniques and stitches. Level 2 patterns offer slightly more complexity, allowing beginners to expand their skills. Level 3 patterns provide a bit more challenge and allow crocheters to showcase their growing expertise.

Before diving into the patterns, the book covers some technical aspects of crochet, including basic counting, understanding the right and wrong side of the fabric, and marking techniques. These skills are essential for following patterns and ensuring your finished projects look their best.

The book provides a comprehensive list of abbreviations commonly used in crochet patterns, ensuring you have a handy reference guide as you work through the projects. Each abbreviation is clearly explained, allowing beginners to familiarize themselves with the terminology.

The book then proceeds to teach the basic stitches used in the patterns, such as the slip knot, chain stitch, slip stitch, double crochet, decrease stitch, fur stitch, and color changes. Step-by-step instructions and accompanying photographs guide you through each stitch, making it easy to learn and practice.

Inside-out techniques are covered in detail, teaching you how to add body details, create chain tails and loops for hair, and properly stuff and sew your crochet animals. Clear instructions and tips ensure that your finished animals are sturdy and well-constructed.

Adding face details is another important aspect of amigurumi. The book provides instructions for sewing on ears, positioning eyes, making noses, and adding other facial features to give your animals their unique personalities.

Washing and safety tips are also included to help you maintain and care for your crocheted animals, ensuring they stay clean and safe for play or display.

The book concludes with variations of the animal patterns, allowing you to add your own creative touch. From cool cats to counting sheep, you'll find inspiration and ideas for customizing your crochet animals.

With its clear instructions, helpful photographs, and beginner-friendly patterns, this book is the perfect companion for anyone eager to start crocheting their own adorable animals. Whether you're new to crochet or looking to expand your skills, this book provides a fun and rewarding journey into the world of amigurumi.

Contents

level 1

The animals in Level 1 require knowledge of only the basics of crochet. They are suitable for beginners who have read the Technicals section.

Emma

The Bunny

Emma is an extremely lovable bunny whose aura is kept in balance by regular dates with her yoga mat. She's a very house-proud mummy rabbit and her warren is her sanctuary. Although often reluctant to tie up her ears and get on with the housework, she does a very fine job once she sets her mind to it. Her creative talents have long slept dormant while other people have become her priority, but it looks as if that might be about to change. Once there's a vase of fresh flowers and a pot of Earl Grey tea brewing on the side, it's time for Emma to get out her needles and create.

You will need

Main colour: Medium
Colour two: Light (scrap)
See also: You Will Need list in Yarns and Other Materials section and Abbreviations.

Body
Work as standard in Medium.

Head
Work as standard in Medium until:
Rnd 6 (Dc5, dc2 into next st)
6 times. (42)
Rnds 7–11 Dc. (5 rnds)
Rnd 12 (Dc5, dc2tog) 6 times. (36)
Rnd 13 Dc.

Rnd 14 (Dc4, dc2tog) 3 times, dc18. (33)
Rnd 15 (Dc3, dc2tog) 3 times, dc18. (30)
Rnd 16 Dc.
Rnd 17 (Dc3, dc2tog) 6 times. (24)
Rnd 18 Dc12, (dc1, dc2tog) 4 times. (20)
Rnd 19 (Dc2, dc2tog) 5 times. (15)
Rnd 20 (Dc2tog) 7 times, dc1. (8)

Ears *(make two)*
Working in Medium, begin by dc6 into ring.
Rnd 1 (Dc1, dc2 into next st)
3 times. (9)
Rnds 2–3 Dc. (2 rnds)
Rnd 4 (Dc2, dc2 into next st)
3 times. (12)
Rnd 5 Dc.
Rnd 6 (Dc3, dc2 into next st)
3 times. (15)
Rnd 7 (Dc2, dc2 into next st)
5 times. (20)
Rnds 8–13 Dc. (6 rnds)
Rnd 14 (Dc3, dc2tog) 4 times. (16)
Rnds 15–16 Dc. (2 rnds)
Rnd 17 (Dc6, dc2tog) twice. (14)
Rnds 18–22 Dc. (5 rnds)
Rnd 23 (Dc5, dc2tog) twice. (12)
Rnds 24–30 Dc. (7 rnds).
Fold flat and dc across the top.

Legs *(make four)*
Work as standard in Medium.

Tail

Working in *Light*, begin by dc6 into ring.
Rnd 1 (Dc2 into next st) 6 times. (12)
Rnd 2 (Dc1, dc2 into next st)
6 times. (18)
Rnds 3–6 Dc. (4 rnds)
Rnd 7 (Dc1, dc2tog) 6 times. (12)
Rnd 8 (Dc2tog) 6 times. (6)

Making Up
See the Stuffing and Sewing and Adding Face Details sections.

Notes
Do not stuff the ears, but do stuff the tail until firm.

Alexandre

The Russian Blue Cat

Lex is convinced that he's one cool cat. He has spent most of the last three years of his life torturing his mother by partaking in the latest fashion trends. He is a self-proclaimed expert in everything a modern teenage boy should be, most notably in the maintenance of his social media profile and taking the best selfie. He is looking forward to learning to drive soon – not because he longs for adventure, but so he no longer has to have his style cramped by the bus. Who knows what the careers advisor might recommend for his future?

You will need

Single colour: Medium
See also: You Will Need list in Yarns and Other Materials section and Abbreviations.

Body
Work as standard.

Head
Work as standard until:
Rnd 6 (Dc5, dc2 into next st)
6 times. (42)
Rnds 7–11 Dc. (5 rnds)
Rnd 12 (Dc5, dc2tog) 6 times. (36)
Rnd 13 (Dc4, dc2tog)
6 times. (30)

Rnd 14 (Dc3, dc2tog) 6 times. (24)
Rnd 15 Dc.
Rnd 16 (Dc1, dc2tog) 8 times. (16)
Rnd 17 Dc.
Rnd 18 (Dc2, dc2tog) 4 times. (12)
Rnd 19 (Dc2tog) 6 times. (6)
Rnd 20 (Dc2tog) 3 times. (3).

Ears *(make two)*
Ch10 and join into circle.
Rnd 1 Dc.
Rnd 2 (Dc2 into next st)
10 times. (20)
Rnds 3–4 Dc. (2 rnds)
Rnd 5 (Dc8, dc2tog) twice. (18)
Rnd 6 (Dc7, dc2tog) twice. (16)
Rnd 7 Dc.
Rnd 8 (Dc6, dc2tog) twice. (14)
Rnd 9 (Dc5, dc2tog) twice. (12)
Rnd 10 (Dc4, dc2tog) twice. (10)
Rnd 11 (Dc3, dc2tog) twice. (8)
Rnd 12 (Dc2, dc2tog) twice. (6)
Rnd 13 (Dc1, dc2tog) twice. (4)
Rnd 14 (Dc4tog) twice. (2)
Rnd 15 Dc4tog.

Legs *(make four)*
Work as standard.

Tail
Begin by dc6 into ring.
Rnds 1–26 Dc.

Making up

See the Stuffing and Sewing and Adding Face Details sections.

Notes

Sew the ears in place on the back of the head by oversewing around the bottom third of the ear, ensuring you can see them from the front.

Piotr

The Polar Bear

Piotr landed the job of his dreams straight out of university. His career as a computer games tester has gone from strength to strength, fuelled by a fast-food diet that is delivered straight to his door. He works from the luxury of his attic in a modest house where the heating is on full-blast all year round, for he really feels the cold. Piotr is kept blindingly white due to his utter aversion to sunshine and not often finding a need to venture out into it. He is one of the best at what he does and is turning the heads that matter, but despite this bear's dedication to his work he still finds time to call his grandma every other day and check how warm her feet are.

You will need

Single colour: Light
See also: You Will Need list in Yarns and Other Materials section and Abbreviations.

Body
Work as standard.

Head
Work as standard until:
Rnd 6 (Dc5, dc2 into next st)
6 times. (42)
Rnds 7–11 Dc. (5 rnds)
Rnd 12 (Dc5, dc2tog) 6 times. (36)
Rnds 13–15 Dc. (3 rnds)

Rnd 16 Dc10, (dc2, dc2tog)
4 times, dc10. (32)
Rnd 17 Dc8, (dc2, dc2tog) 4 times, dc8. (28)
Rnd 18 Dc6, (dc2, dc2tog) 4 times, dc6. (24)
Rnd 19 Dc4, (dc2, dc2tog) 4 times, dc4. (20)
Rnd 20 Dc4, (dc1, dc2tog) 4 times, dc4. (16)
Rnd 21 Dc.
Rnd 22 Dc4, (dc2tog) 4 times, dc4. (12)
Rnd 23 (Dc2tog) 6 times. (6)

Ears *(make two)*
Begin by dc6 into ring.
Rnd 1 (Dc2 into next st)
6 times. (12)
Rnds 2–5 Dc. (4 rnds)
Rnd 6 (Dc2tog) 6 times. (6)

Legs *(make four)*
Work as standard.

Tail
Begin by dc6 into ring.
Rnd 1 (Dc2 into next st)
6 times. (12)
Rnds 2–3 Dc. (2 rnds)
Rnd 4 (Dc2tog) 6 times. (6)
Rnd 5 (Dc2tog) 3 times. (3)

Making Up
See the Stuffing and Sewing and Adding Face Details sections.

Bridget

The Elephant

Bridget has a sweet tooth. More than anything else in the world she loves baking cakes, and scones, and cookies and more cakes... but especially custard tarts. As a young elephant she would spend hours having tea parties with her dolls and she never really grew out of it. Nowadays, her idea of a good party is a baby shower: the glory of baking the best cake, no pressure to swap her cup and saucer for a wine glass, and lots and lots of baby chat. One day she'll make the best mummy a calf could hope for, but for now she's determined to stay focused on tomorrow's diet and meeting the man of her dreams.

You will need

Single colour: Medium
See also: You Will Need list in Yarns and Other Materials section and Abbreviations.

Body
Work as standard.

Head
Work as standard until:
Rnd 6 (Dc5, dc2 into next st)
6 times. (42)
Rnds 7–11 Dc. (5 rnds)
Rnd 12 (Dc5, dc2tog) 6 times. (36)
Rnd 13 Dc.
Rnd 14 (Dc4, dc2tog) 3 times, dc18. (33)

Rnd 15 (Dc3, dc2tog) 3 times, dc18. (30)
Rnd 16 Dc.
Rnd 17 (Dc3, dc2tog) 6 times. (24)
Rnd 18 Dc12, (dc1, dc2tog)
4 times. (20)
Rnd 19 (Dc2, dc2tog) 5 times. (15)
Rnds 20–22 Dc. (3 rnds)
Rnd 23 (Dc1, dc2tog) 5 times. (10)
Rnds 24–33 Dc. (10 rnds)
Stuff the head only and then sew the trunk closed flat.

Ears *(make two)*
Work as standard until:
Rnd 7 (Dc6, dc2 into next st)
6 times. (48)
Fold in half and dc around edge to join.

Legs *(make four)*
Begin by dc6 into ring.
Rnd 1 (Dc2 into next st)
6 times. (12)
Rnd 2 (Dc1, dc2 into next st)
6 times. (18)
Rnd 3 (Dc2, dc2 into next st)
6 times. (24)
Rnds 4–6 Dc. (3 rnds)
Rnd 7 (Dc1, dc2tog) 8 times. (16)
Rnd 8 (Dc2, dc2tog) 4 times. (12)
Rnds 9–24 Dc. (16 rnds)

Tail
Using four strands of the yarn held together, ch6 big sts then work
three ch10 loops onto the end.

Making Up
See the Stuffing and Sewing and Adding Face Details sections.

Notes
Although it is tempting to stuff the trunk, it looks best unstuffed in the same way as the legs.

Simon

The Sheep

Simon is a meticulous bachelor with little in his life to worry about. Following a minor hiccup a few years back, he swapped his overstretched mortgage for a red sports car, downsized to somewhere with a plasma TV bigger than the bathroom, and learned to wakeboard. Life as a dentist has never been a bad one; it gives Simon plenty of time to keep on top of his appearance, including the opportunity to check out how well trimmed his eyebrows are in the reflection of his customers' highly polished teeth. The future looks bright for a sheep who now has no need ever to learn how to boil an egg.

You will need

Single colour: Light
See also: You Will Need list in Yarns and Other Materials section
and Abbreviations.

Body
Work as standard.

Head
Work as standard until:
Rnd 6 (Dc5, dc2 into next st) 6 times. (42)
Rnds 7–11 Dc. (5 rnds)
Rnd 12 (Dc5, dc2tog) 6 times. (36)
Rnds 13–14 Dc. (2 rnds)
Rnd 15 Dc4, (dc2tog) 3 times, dc26. (33)

Rnd 16 Dc3, (dc2tog) 3 times, dc24. (30)
Rnd 17 Dc.
Rnd 18 (Dc3, dc2tog) 6 times. (24)
Rnds 19–21 Dc. (3 rnds)
Rnd 22 (Dc2, dc2tog) 6 times. (18)
Rnd 23 Dc.
Rnd 24 (Dc1, dc2tog) 6 times. (12)
Rnd 25 (Dc2tog) 6 times. (6)

Ears *(make two)*
Begin by dc6 into ring.
Rnd 1 (Dc2 into next st) 6 times. (12)
Rnds 2–5 Dc. (4 rnds)
Rnd 6 (Dc2tog) 6 times. (6)

Legs *(make four)*
Work as standard.

Tail
Begin by dc6 into ring.
Rnd 1 (Dc2 into next st)
6 times. (12)
Rnds 2–4 Dc. (3 rnds)
Rnd 5 (Dc2tog) 6 times. (6)
Rnd 6 Dc.

Fleece
Work ch8 loops all over the body, leaving the bottom where the legs are attached plain to ensure balance when sitting.

Making Up
See the Stuffing and Sewing and Adding Face Details sections.

Notes

Sew on all parts before working the fleece.

Georgina

The Hippo

Georgina is a princess among hippos. Despite her PhD in something very scientific with a title that has an acronym longer than her name, her brain feels most tested when she is trying out the latest nail-art techniques on a Friday night. An evening in with takeaway sushi and reality TV is her perfect antidote to a stressful week in the office. She is fiercely loyal, a friend to everyone, and with never a whine, moan or grumble she is by far one of the most positive animals around the watering hole.

You will need

Single colour: Medium
See also: You Will Need list in Yarns and Other Materials section and Abbreviations.

Body
Work as standard.

Head
Work as standard until:
Rnd 3 (Dc2, dc2 into next st) 6 times. (24)
Rnds 4–8 Dc. (5 rnds)
Rnd 9 (Dc2, dc2tog) 6 times. (18)
Rnd 10 (Dc1, dc2 into next st) 9 times. (27)
Rnd 11 Dc.
Rnd 12 (Dc8, dc2 into next st) 3 times. (30)
Rnd 13 (Dc9, dc2 into next st) 3 times. (33)

Rnd 14 (Dc10, dc2 into next st)
3 times. (36)
Rnd 15 (Dc11, dc2 into next st) 3 times. (39)
Rnd 16 (Dc12, dc2 into next st) 3 times. (42)
Rnd 17 Dc.
Rnd 18 (Dc1, dc2tog) 14 times. (28)
Rnd 19 (Dc5, dc2tog) 4 times. (24)
Rnd 20 (Dc2, dc2tog) 6 times. (18)

Ears *(make two)*
Begin by dc6 into ring.
Rnd 1 (Dc2 into next st) 6 times. (12)
Rnds 2–5 Dc. (4 rnds)
Rnd 6 (Dc2tog) 6 times. (6)

Legs *(make four)*
Begin by dc6 into ring.
Rnd 1 (Dc2 into next st) 6 times. (12)
Rnd 2 (Dc1, dc2 into next st) 6 times. (18)
Rnd 3 (Dc2, dc2 into next st) 6 times. (24)
Rnds 4–6 Dc. (3 rnds)
Rnd 7 (Dc1, dc2tog) 8 times. (16)
Rnd 8 (Dc2, dc2tog) 4 times. (12)
Rnds 9–24 Dc. (16 rnds)

Tail
Using four strands of the yarn held together, ch8 big sts then work three ch10 loops onto the end.

Nostrils *(make two)*
Make a foundation ring and then sew it into position on the top of the nose.

Making Up
See the Stuffing and Sewing and Adding Face Details sections.

Seamus

The Alpaca

Seamus fancies himself as an actor. The only major downside of boasting a face that's good enough to pull off any type of hat is that you are continually fighting a battle with the unruly hair that sits beneath it. Seamus has been the lead in his village's Amateur Dramatic Society for the last 25 years, and that has only accelerated the growth of his larger-than-life character. No one can deny the power and depth of his singing voice; every day it can be heard bellowing from the open windows of his thatched cottage in accompaniment to the dawn chorus.

You will need

Single colour: Dark
See also: You Will Need list in Yarns and Other Materials section
and Abbreviations.

Body
Work as standard until:
Rnd 21 (Dc2, dc2tog) 6 times. (24)
Rnds 22–29 Dc. (8 rnds)
Rnd 30 (Dc2, dc2tog) 6 times. (18)
Rnds 31–34 Dc. (4 rnds)
Rnd 35 (Dc2tog) 9 times. (9)

Head
Work as standard until:
Rnd 6 (Dc5, dc2 into next st) 6 times. (42)

Rnds 7–11 Dc. (5 rnds)
Rnd 12 (Dc5, dc2tog) 6 times. (36)
Rnd 13 Dc.
Rnd 14 (Dc4, dc2tog) 6 times. (30)
Rnd 15 (Dc3, dc2tog) 6 times. (24)
Rnds 16–18 Dc. (3 rnds)
Rnd 19 (Dc4, dc2tog) 4 times. (20)
Rnd 20 (Dc3, dc2tog) 4 times. (16)
Rnds 21–22 Dc. (2 rnds)
Rnd 23 (Dc2tog) 8 times. (8)
Rnd 24 Dc.

Ears *(make two)*
Begin by dc6 into ring.
Rnd 1 (Dc2 into next st)
6 times. (12)
Rnd 2 (Dc1, dc2 into next st) 6 times. (18)
Rnds 3–4 Dc. (2 rnds)
Rnd 5 (Dc1, dc2tog) 6 times. (12)
Rnd 6 Dc.
Rnd 7 (Dc2tog) 6 times. (6)

Legs *(make four)*
Work as standard.

Tail
Begin by dc6 into ring.
Rnd 1 (Dc2 into next st)
6 times. (12)
Rnds 2–5 Dc. (4 rnds)
Rnd 6 (Dc2tog) 6 times. (6)

Top Knot

Cover the top of the head in ch8 loops with a row of densely packed ch10 fur loops at the front between the ears to create a fringe.

Making Up
See the Stuffing and Sewing and Adding Face Details sections.

Austin

The Rhino

Austin is a high-flying rhino. A private airline pilot with four daughters and a glamorous wife to keep in Jimmy Choos, he is a proud and hard-working father. When he's not in the captain's chair he's on the rowing machine in the gym or stretching his legs at breakneck speeds around the local park. He and his wife are often seen at the most high-falutin' cocktail bars in the world, easily recognized by their immaculately dyed hair, raucous laughter and the light glinting off their French-polished horns.

You will need

Main colour: Dark
Colour two: Light (scrap)
See also: You Will Need list in Yarns and Other Materials section and Abbreviations.

Body
Work as standard in *Dark*.

Head
Work as standard in *Dark* until:
Rnd 6 (Dc5, dc2 into next st) 6 times. (42)
Rnds 7–11 Dc. (5 rnds)
Rnd 12 (Dc5, dc2tog) 6 times. (36)
Rnd 13 (Dc4, dc2tog) 6 times. (30)
Rnd 14 (Dc3, dc2tog) 6 times. (24)
Rnd 15 Dc12, (dc1, dc2tog) 4 times. (20)

Rnds 16–18 Dc. (3 rnds)
Rnd 19 (Dc3, dc2 into next st) 5 times. (25)
Rnds 20–22 Dc. (3 rnds)
Rnd 23 (Dc3, dc2tog) 5 times. (20)
Rnd 24 (Dc2, dc2tog) 5 times. (15)
Rnd 25 (Dc1, dc2tog) 5 times. (10)
Rnd 26 (Dc2tog) 5 times. (5)

Ears *(make two)*
Working in *Dark*, begin by dc6 into ring.
Rnd 1 (Dc2 into next st)
6 times. (12)
Rnds 2–5 Dc. (4 rnds)
Rnd 6 (Dc2tog) 6 times. (6)

Legs *(make four)*
Working in *Dark*, begin by dc6 into ring.
Rnd 1 (Dc2 into next st)
6 times. (12)
Rnd 2 (Dc1, dc2 into next st) 6 times. (18)
Rnd 3 (Dc2, dc2 into next st) 6 times. (24)
Rnds 4–6 Dc. (3 rnds)
Rnd 7 (Dc1, dc2tog) 8 times. (16)
Rnd 8 (Dc2, dc2tog) 4 times. (12)
Rnds 9–24 Dc. (16 rnds)

Tail
Working in *Dark* and using four strands of the yarn held together,
ch8 big sts.

Horn
Working in *Light*, ch12 and sl st to join into circle.
Rnd 1 Dc.

Rnd 2 Dc10, dc2tog. (11)
Rnd 3 Dc9, dc2tog. (10)
Rnd 4 Dc8, dc2tog. (9)
Rnd 5 Dc7, dc2tog. (8)
Rnd 6 Dc6, dc2tog. (7)
Rnd 7 Dc5, dc2tog. (6)
Rnd 8 Dc4, dc2tog. (5)
Rnd 9 Dc3, dc2tog. (4)
Rnd 10 Dc2, dc2tog. (3)
Rnd 11 Dc3tog.

Making Up
See the Stuffing and Sewing and Adding Face Details sections.

Notes
Stuff the horn firmly before sewing into position, curving it towards the forehead.

Rufus

The Lion

Rufus is a bad plumber. His blindness to this fact has landed him in several very wet scenarios. Some of his most spectacularly disastrous incidents have included falling through a ceiling while clinging for dear life onto a water tank; calling the fire brigade to assist with his own tail being caught in a sink; and causing a large electrical explosion while installing a dehumidifier in his own very small cellar. He is well-intentioned in his sales pitch, but was perhaps sleeping through at least half of his night classes and got very lucky in his final exam. Thankfully, he came to the trade late in life after abandoning a successful career in daytime sales television, so retirement is just around the corner.

You will need

Main colour: Medium
Colour two: Dark
See also: You Will Need list in Yarns and Other Materials section
   and Abbreviations.

Body
Work as standard in Medium.

Head
Work as standard in Medium until:
Rnd 6 (Dc5, dc2 into next st) 6 times. (42)
Rnds 7–11 Dc. (5 rnds)

Rnd 12 Dc10, dc2tog, dc5, dc2tog, dc10, dc2tog, dc5, dc2tog, dc4. (38)
Rnd 13 Dc14, dc2tog, dc6, dc2tog, dc14. (36)
Rnd 14 (Dc4, dc2tog) 6 times. (30)
Rnd 15 (Dc3, dc2tog) 6 times. (24)
Rnd 16 Dc9, dc2tog, dc2, dc2tog, dc9. (22)
Rnd 17 Dc7, dc2tog, dc2, dc2tog, dc9. (20)
Rnds 18–23 Dc. (5 rnds)
Rnd 24 (Dc2tog) 10 times. (10)
Rnd 25 (Dc2tog) 5 times. (5)

Ears *(make two)*
Working in Medium, begin by dc6 into ring.
Rnd 1 (Dc2 into next st)
6 times. (12)
Rnd 2 (Dc1, dc2 into next st) 6 times. (18)
Rnds 3–5 Dc. (3 rnds)
Rnd 6 (Dc1, dc2tog). (12)
Rnd 7 (Dc2tog) 6 times. (6)

Legs *(make four)*
Work as standard in Medium.

Tail
Working in Medium and using four strands of the yarn held together, ch18 big sts. Attach six ch10 loops to end in *Dark*.

Mane
Working in *Dark*, cover the whole top of the head in 10st chain loops with three 15st chain loops under the chin for a beard.

Making Up
See the Stuffing and Sewing and Adding Face Details sections.

Notes
Don't build the chains too close for the mane or your lion will become so top-heavy that even the tummy won't help him to balance!

Richard

The Large White Pig

Richard does not have a mobile phone. He is a neo-luddite rooted firmly in his allotment, reading the daily newspaper from the back page forwards. He was once quite a soccer player, but hung up his studs for slippers just before the glamour arrived in the business. The internet remains a mystery to him despite countless well-meaning grandchildren enrolling him on courses and classes. His great-grandchildren love their 'GGpig' and his funny ways, and still fear going in goal against the golden trotter.

You will need

Single colour: Light
See also: You Will Need list in Yarns and Other Materials section and Abbreviations.

Body
Work as standard.

Head
Work as standard until:
Rnd 6 (Dc5, dc2 in next st) 6 times. (42)
Rnds 7–11 Dc. (5 rnds)
Rnd 12 (Dc5, dc2tog) 6 times. (36)
Rnd 13 Dc.
Rnd 14 (Dc4, dc2tog) 3 times, dc18. (33)
Rnd 15 (Dc3, dc2tog) 3 times, dc18. (30)
Rnd 16 Dc.

Rnd 17 (Dc3, dc2tog) 6 times. (24)
Rnd 18 Dc12, (dc1, dc2tog) 4 times. (20)
Rnd 19 (Dc2, dc2tog) 5 times. (15)
Rnds 20–21 Dc. (2 rnds)
Rnd 22 (Dc1, dc2tog) 5 times. (10)
Rnd 23 (Dc2tog) 5 times. (5)

Ears *(make two)*
Work as standard until:
Rnd 4 (Dc3, dc2 into next st) 6 times. (30 sts)

Legs *(make four)* **Work as standard.**

Tail
Ch10, then turn and work dc2 into every stitch back along (20).

Making Up
See the Stuffing and Sewing and Adding Face Details sections.

Notes
To finish the ears, fold the circles in half RS out and dc halfway around the semi-circle before opening this up and sewing into position with the points forwards.

40

level 2

Level 2 animals introduce simple shade changing. Cut your yarn after the change. You don't need to worry about tying in the ends; just leave them inside the part. In addition, some of the organic shapes have been made using a free-form style of crochet; rather than the pattern being stated in rounds it will give the instruction for the whole piece as if it were one big round.

Germaine

The Gorilla

Germaine is an OAG with attitude. She's everyone's surrogate grandma; she has a toy box full of wonders that she has collected over 60 years of babysitting and that has fired the imagination of hundreds of children. Her blue eyeshadow tells of an undying pride in her appearance and is so thick on her eyelids that many debate as to whether she ever washes it off. To keep herself in shape she marches over five miles a day looking through the neighbours' windows, always perfectly made-up, with her trousers tucked into her socks and a rain cap on.

You will need

Main colour: Dark

Colour two: Medium
See also: You Will Need list in Yarns and Other Materials section
and Abbreviations.

Body
Work as standard in *Dark*.

Head
Work as standard in *Dark* until:
Rnd 6 (Dc5, dc2 into next st) 6 times. (42)
Rnds 7–11 Dc. (5 rnds)
Rnd 12 (Dc5, dc2tog) 6 times. (36)
Rnd 13 Dc.
Rnd 14 (Dc4, dc2tog) 3 times, dc18. (33)
Rnd 15 (Dc3, dc2tog) 3 times, dc18. (30)
Rnd 16 Dc.
Rnd 17 (Dc3, dc2tog) 6 times. (24)
Rnd 18 Dc12, (dc1, dc2tog) 4 times. (20)
Rnd 19 (Dc2, dc2tog) 5 times. (15)
Rnd 20 (Dc2tog) 7 times, dc1. (8)

Muzzle
Work as standard in Medium until:
Rnd 3 (Dc2, dc2 into next st) 6 times. (24 sts)
Rnds 4–6 Dc. (3 rnds).

Ears *(make two)*
Working in Medium, begin by dc6 into ring.
Rnd 1 (Dc2 into next st) 6 times. (12)
Rnd 2–4 Dc. (3 rnds)
Rnd 5 (Dc2tog) 6 times. (6)

Legs *(make four)*

Work two as standard in Medium, changing to *Dark* at Rnd 8.
Work two in the same way but continuing length by 6 rnds (to Rnd 30).

Eye PATCH
Working in Medium, ch16 and sl st to join into circle.
Rnd 1 (Dc2 into next st) 4 times, dc4, (dc2 into next st) 4 times, dc4.
Sew the circle across to form a 'mask' shape with two rounded ends.

Making Up
See the Stuffing and Sewing and Adding Face Details sections.

Notes
Stuff the muzzle and sew into place with the eye patch just above.
Work 3 ch10 loops on the top of the head around one stitch to create a tuft.

44

Winston

The Aardvark

Winston has four pet cats. He possesses a natural ability to make everyone smile with his ridiculously big grin that always quickly follows 'good morning', 'good afternoon' and 'good evening'. Other than tending to his pets and working towards his grade 8 saxophone exam, he spends his spare time on the indoor ski slope. He hits the Alps three times a year clad in the same gear he's been wearing for far too many seasons. But if anyone's going to pull off a faded vintage onesie at 70 miles an hour, it's this innately cool aardvark.

You will need

Main colour: Dark
Colour two: Medium
See also: You Will Need list in Yarns and Other Materials section and Abbreviations.

Body
Work as standard in *Dark*.

Head
Work as standard in Medium until:
Rnd 6 (Dc5, dc2 into next st)
6 times. (42)
Rnds 7–11 Dc. (5 rnds)
Rnd 12 (Dc5, dc2tog) 6 times. (36)
Rnd 13 (Dc4, dc2tog)
6 times. (30)

Rnd 14 Dc.
Rnd 15 (Dc3, dc2tog) 6 times. (24)
Rnd 16 Dc.
Rnd 17 (Dc2, dc2tog) 6 times. (18)
Rnds 18–24 Dc. (7 rnds)
Rnd 25 (Dc1, dc2tog) 6 times. (12)
Rnds 26–28 Dc. (3 rnds)
Rnd 29 (Dc1, dc2 into next st)
6 times. (18)
Do not gather sts.

Ears *(make two)*
Working in Medium, ch10 and join into circle.
Rnds 1–4 Dc. (4 rnds)
Rnd 5 (Dc4, dc2 into next st) twice. (12)
Rnd 6 Dc.
Rnd 7 (Dc5, dc2 into next st) twice. (14)
Rnds 8–10 Dc. (3 rnds)
Rnd 11 (Dc5, dc2tog) twice. (12)
Rnd 12 (Dc4, dc2tog) twice. (10)
Rnd 13 (Dc3, dc2tog) twice. (8)
Rnd 14 (Dc2, dc2tog) twice. (6)
Rnd 15 Dc.
Rnd 16 (Dc2tog) 3 times. (3)
Rnd 17 Dc3tog.

Legs *(make four)*
Work as standard in Medium, changing to *Dark* at Rnd 3.

Tail
Work in free-form style without rounds in Medium: ch12 and sl st to
join into circle, dc36, dc2tog, dc30, dc2tog, dc30, dc2tog, dc20,
dc2tog, dc15, dc2tog, dc15 dc2tog, dc2tog to a point.

Making Up
See the Stuffing and Sewing and Adding Face Details sections.

Notes

Stuff the head and then close it off by rolling back the 'trunk' and dc a round of sts into the trunk sts two rows back from end. Gather these sts to close off the trunk. Stuff the tail firmly so it stands out from the body and then sew into position on the back.

Penelope

The Bear

Penelope is a career bear at the top of her game. She expresses herself with her very extensive and obscenely expensive shoe collection. Possessing a very powerful blue-sky brain, she is a workaholic who gets results and brings out the best in any team she leads. Her signature drink is a complex champagne cocktail that no barman has ever heard of, but she is no party animal and has a reputation for always being the first to leave having secretly paid the whole bill. Her partner is equally impressive character, and together they will scuba dive the world.

You will need

Main colour: Dark
Colour two: Light
See also: You Will Need list in Yarns and Other Materials section
   and Abbreviations.

Body
Work as standard in *Dark*.

Head
Work as standard in *Dark* until:
Rnd 6 (Dc5, dc2 into next st) 6 times. (42)
Rnds 7–11 Dc. (5 rnds)
Rnd 12 (Dc5, dc2tog) 6 times. (36)
Rnds 13–15 Dc. (3 rnds)
Rnd 16 Dc10, (dc2, dc2tog) 4 times, dc10. (32)

Rnd 17 Dc8, (dc2, dc2tog) 4 times, dc8. (28)
Change to *Light*.
Rnd 18 Dc6, (dc2, dc2tog) 4 times, dc6. (24)
Rnd 19 Dc4, (dc2, dc2tog) 4 times, dc4. (20)
Rnd 20 Dc4, (dc1, dc2tog) 4 times, dc4. (16)
Rnd 21 Dc.
Rnd 22 Dc4, (dc2tog) 4 times, dc4. (12)
Rnd 23 (Dc2tog) 6 times. (6)

Ears *(make two)*
Working in *Dark*, begin by dc6 into ring.
Rnd 1 (Dc2 into next st)
6 times. (12)
Rnds 2–5 Dc. (4 rnds)
Rnd 6 (Dc2tog) 6 times. (6)

Legs *(make four)*
Work as standard in *Dark*.

Tail
Working in *Dark*, begin by dc6 into ring.
Rnd 1 (Dc2 into next st) 6 times. (12)
Rnds 2–3 Dc. (2 rnds)
Rnd 4 (Dc2tog) 6 times. (6)
Rnd 5 (Dc2tog) 3 times. (3)

Making Up
See the Stuffing and Sewing and Adding Face Details sections.

Hank

The Dorset Down Sheep

Hank is a seriously well-travelled ram with a ewe on every farm. Even as a newborn lamb he possessed a charm that melted all the midwives, and in his life he has continued to win the heart of every woman who crosses his path. He's a smooth-talking stud of a sheep who carries his twelve-string guitar on his back wherever he goes. Every year his fleece gets hand-spun by his grandmother and knitted up into an intricate Aran jumper that keeps him warm through the unpredictable British summers.

You will need

Main colour: Light
Colour two: Dark
See also: You Will Need list in Yarns and Other Materials section and Abbreviations.

Body
Work as standard in *Light*.

Head
Work as standard in *Light* until:
Rnd 6 (Dc5, dc2 into next st) 6 times. (42)
Rnds 7–11 Dc. (5 rnds)
Rnd 12 (Dc5, dc2tog) 6 times. (36)
Rnds 13–14 Dc. (2 rnds)
Rnd 15 Dc4, (dc2tog) 3 times, dc26. (33)
Rnd 16 Dc3, (dc2tog) 3 times, dc24. (30)

Rnd 17 Dc.
Rnd 18 (Dc3, dc2tog) 6 times. (24)
Change to *Dark*.
Rnds 19–21 Dc. (3 rnds)
Rnd 22 (Dc2, dc2tog) 6 times. (18)
Rnd 23 Dc.
Rnd 24 (Dc1, dc2tog) 6 times. (12)
Rnd 25 (Dc2tog) 6 times. (6)

Ears *(make two)*
Working in *Dark*, begin by dc6 into ring.
Rnd 1 (Dc2 into next st) 6 times. (12)
Rnds 2–5 Dc. (4 rnds)
Rnd 6 (Dc2tog) 6 times. (6)

Legs *(make four)*
Work as standard in *Dark*.

Tail
Working in *Light*, begin by dc6 into ring.
Rnd 1 (Dc2 into next st) 6 times. (12)
Rnds 2–4 Dc. (3 rnds)
Rnd 5 (Dc2tog) 6 times. (6)
Rnd 6 Dc.

Fleece
Working in *Light*, work ch8 loops all over the body and head with the exception of the 'nose'. Swap to ch4 loops at the bottom of the body to ensure balance when sitting.

Making Up
See the Stuffing and Sewing and Adding Face Details sections.

Notes

Sew on all parts before working the fleece.

Fiona

The Panda

Fiona is a student. One thing this very brainy panda has never turned her mind to during her three years at university is the development of time-management skills good enough to keep her on top of her laundry pile. Only when her chest of drawers stands empty and she is clothed in someone else's borrowed pyjamas will she contemplate hauling a month's worth of clothes to the launderette for a full day of washing and drying. She applies a similar philosophy to her crockery, and is frequently caught microwaving noodles in her teapot before reaching for the washing-up liquid.

You will need

Main colour: Dark
Colour two: Light
See also: You Will Need list in Yarns and Other Materials section
   and Abbreviations.

Body
Work as standard in *Light* and change to *Dark* in the middle of Rnd 17.

Head
Work as standard in *Light* until:
Rnd 6 (Dc5, dc2 into next st) 6 times. (42)
Rnds 7–11 Dc. (5 rnds)
Rnd 12 (Dc5, dc2tog) 6 times. (36)
Rnds 13–15 Dc. (3 rnds)

Rnd 16 Dc10, (dc2, dc2tog) 4 times, dc10. (32)
Rnd 17 Dc8, (dc2, dc2tog) 4 times, dc8. (28)
Rnd 18 Dc6, (dc2, dc2tog) 4 times, dc6. (24)
Rnd 19 Dc4, (dc2, dc2tog) 4 times, dc4. (20)
Rnd 20 Dc4, (dc1, dc2tog) 4 times, dc4. (16)
Rnd 21 Dc.
Rnd 22 Dc4, (dc2tog) 4 times, dc4. (12)
Rnd 23 (Dc2tog) 6 times. (6)

Ears *(make two)*
Working in *Dark*, begin by dc6 into ring.
Rnd 1 (Dc2 into next st) 6 times. (12)
Rnds 2–5 Dc. (4 rnds)
Rnd 6 (Dc2tog) 6 times. (6)

Legs *(make four)*
Work as standard in *Dark*.

Tail
Working in *Light*, begin by dc6 into ring.
Rnd 1 (Dc2 into next st) 6 times. (12)
Rnds 2–3 Dc. (2 rnds)
Rnd 4 (Dc2tog) 6 times. (6)
Rnd 5 (Dc2tog) 3 times. (3)

Eye Patches *(make two)*
Working in *Dark*, begin by dc6 into ring.
Rnd 1 (Dc2 into next st) 6 times. (12)

Making Up
See the Stuffing and Sewing and Adding Face Details sections.

Juno

The Siamese Cat

Juno spends her days listening to other people's problems; then she spends most evenings taking her problems out on other people. Many underestimate this dainty cat's mastery of the martial arts, and that inevitably lands them on their back with little idea of how they got there. Each night after a heavy training session, or the defeat of yet another opponent, she collapses onto her oversized cream leather sofa and laps up a White Russian and the latest prize-winning novel or two.

You will need

Main colour: Light
Colour two: Dark
See also: You Will Need list in Yarns and Other Materials section and Abbreviations.

Body
Work as standard in *Light*.

Head
Work as standard in *Light* until:
Rnd 6 (Dc5, dc2 into next st) 6 times. (42)
Rnds 7–11 Dc. (5 rnds)
Rnd 12 (Dc5, dc2tog) 6 times. (36)
Rnd 13 (Dc4, dc2tog) 6 times. (30)
Rnd 14 (Dc3, dc2tog) 6 times. (24)
Rnd 15 Dc.

Change to *Dark*.
Rnd 16 (Dc1, dc2tog) 8 times. (16)
Rnd 17 Dc.
Rnd 18 (Dc2, dc2tog) 4 times. (12)
Rnd 19 (Dc2tog) 6 times. (6)
Rnd 20 (Dc2tog) 3 times. (3)

Ears *(make two)*
Working in *Dark*, ch10 and sl st to join into circle.
Rnd 1 Dc.
Rnd 2 (Dc2 into next st)
10 times. (20)
Rnds 3–4 Dc. (2 rnds)
Rnd 5 (Dc8, dc2tog) twice. (18)
Rnd 6 (Dc7, dc2tog) twice. (16)
Rnd 7 Dc.
Rnd 8 (Dc6, dc2tog) twice. (14)
Rnd 9 (Dc5, dc2tog) twice. (12)
Rnd 10 Dc.
Rnd 11 (Dc4, dc2tog) twice. (10)
Rnd 12 Dc.
Rnd 13 (Dc3, dc2tog) twice. (8)
Rnd 14 (Dc2, dc2tog) twice. (6)
Rnd 15 (Dc1, dc2tog) twice. (4)
Rnd 16 Dc4tog.

Legs *(make four)*
Work as standard in *Dark*, changing to *Light* at Rnd 10.

Tail
Working in *Dark*, begin by dc8 into ring.
Rnds 1–26 Dc.

Making Up
See the Stuffing and Sewing and Adding Face Details sections.

Notes
Sew the ears in place on the back of the head by oversewing around the bottom third of the ear, ensuring you can see them from the front.

Angharad

The Donkey

Angharad is a surfer. In her VW camper she travels the south coast of the UK chasing waves in all seasons. A seaside donkey who never got over the feel of the sand and the taste of salt, she's enjoying her retirement in a wetsuit with no obligation to carry children around. She takes her cream tea with the jam first and is mortally offended if it's raspberry not strawberry. She is a collector of shells and unusual stones and can always be caught on the beach with her ass in the air happily minding her own business.

You will need

Main colour: Dark
Colour two: Light
See also: You Will Need list in Yarns and Other Materials section and Abbreviations.

Body
Work as standard in *Dark*.

Head
Begin in *Dark* as standard until:
Rnd 6 (Dc5, dc2 into next st) 6 times. (42)
Rnds 7–12 Dc. (6 rnds)
Rnd 13 (Dc5, dc2tog) 6 times. (36)
Rnd 14 (Dc1, dc2tog) 12 times. (24)
Rnd 15 (Dc2, dc2tog) 6 times. (18)
Change to *Light*.

Rnds 16–22 Dc. (7 rnds)
Rnd 23 (Dc1, dc2tog) 6 times. (12)
Rnd 24 (Dc2tog) 6 times. (6)

Ears *(make two)*

Working in *Dark*, ch20 and sl st to join into circle.
Rnd 1 (Dc8, dc2tog) twice. (18)
Rnd 2 Dc.
Rnd 3 (Dc7, dc2tog) twice. (16)
Rnds 4–7 Dc. (4 rnds)
Rnd 8 (Dc6, dc2tog) twice. (14)
Rnd 9 Dc.
Rnd 10 (Dc5, dc2tog) twice. (12)
Rnd 11 (Dc2, dc2tog) 3 times. (9)
Rnd 12 (Dc1, dc2tog) 3 times. (6)
Rnd 13 (Dc2tog) 3 times. (3)

Legs *(make four)*

Work as standard in *Light*, changing to *Dark* at Rnd 9.

Tail

Working in *Dark* and using four strands of the yarn held together, ch8 big sts. Attach three ch15 loops to end.

Mane

In *Dark* work a mane up the back of the head with ch12 loops. Add more between the ears to create a fringe.

Making Up

See the Stuffing and Sewing and Adding Face Details sections.

Benedict

The Chimpanzee

Show-off Benedict hasn't stopped raving since the early 1990s and is never happier than when throwing shapes in the centre of a circle. He has a cheesy grin and a fixed thousand-yard stare that is only broken in the frenzied ten minutes in which he needs to purchase next year's Glastonbury ticket. His wardrobe principally consists of a wide selection of neon bobble hats and flip-flops, which he supplements with various sweaty band T-shirts that he picks up on his travels. That said, in his job as head gardener at a stately home, he has won awards for his topiary maze design (and the plants don't care what he wears).

You will need

Main colour: Dark
Colour two: Light
See also: You Will Need list in Yarns and Other Materials section and Abbreviations.

Body
Work as standard in *Dark*.

Head
Work as standard in *Dark* until:
Rnd 6 (Dc5, dc2 into next st) 6 times. (42)
Rnds 7–11 Dc. (5 rnds)
Rnd 12 (Dc5, dc2tog) 6 times. (36)
Rnd 13 Dc.

Rnd 14 (Dc4, dc2tog) 3 times, dc18. (33)
Rnd 15 (Dc3, dc2tog) 3 times, dc18. (30)
Rnd 16 Dc.
Rnd 17 (Dc3, dc2tog) 6 times. (24)
Rnd 18 Dc12, (dc1, dc2tog) 4 times. (20)
Rnd 19 (Dc2, dc2tog) 5 times. (15)
Rnd 20 (Dc2tog) 7 times, dc1. (8)

Muzzle
Work as standard in *Light* until:
Rnd 3 (Dc2, dc2tog into next st) 6 times. (24 sts)
Rnds 4–7 Dc. (4 rnds)

Ears *(make two)*
Working in *Light*, begin by dc4 into ring.
Rnd 1 (Dc2 into next st) 4 times. (8)
Rnd 2 (Dc2 into next st) 8 times. (16)
Rnds 3–4 Dc. (2 rnds)
Rnd 5 (Dc2tog) 8 times. (8)
Rnd 6 (Dc2tog) 4 times. (4)

Legs *(make four)*
Work two as standard in *Light*, changing to *Dark* at Rnd 3.
Work two as standard with colour change as for first two legs but continuing length by 6 rnds (to Rnd 30) (these legs become the 'arms').

Eye Patches *(make two)*
Working in *Light*, begin by dc6 into ring.
Rnd 1 (Dc2 into next st) 6 times. (12)

Making Up
See the Stuffing and Sewing and Adding Face Details sections.

Stuff the muzzle and sew into place with the eye patches just above. Flatten the ears so the foundation ring is in the centre of the ear and sew into position.

Samuel

The Koala

Samuel went on a gap year at the turn of the millennium and has never come back. In his travels around Europe he has become fluent in five languages and, as a current resident of Asia, has never tired of eating dim sum for breakfast. He has no place to call his own but instead keeps moving around; his home is wherever he takes his trainers off. He is a self-proclaimed artist who would maybe have something to show off, but he keeps losing track of his sketchbooks. Perhaps one day he will finally 'find himself' (and some drawings) in a bowl of pho soup and blow us all away with the talent he's been assuring us he has.

You will need

Main colour: Medium
Colour two: Dark (scrap)
Colour three: Light (scrap)
See also: You Will Need list in Yarns and Other Materials section and Abbreviations.

Body
Work as standard in Medium.

Head
Work as standard in Medium until:
Rnd 7 (Dc6, dc2 into next st) 6 times. (48)
Rnds 8–12 Dc. (5 rnds)
Rnd 13 (Dc4, dc2tog) 8 times. (40)

Rnd 14 Dc.
Rnd 15 Dc20, (dc1, dc2tog) 5 times, dc5. (35)
Rnd 16 Dc20, (dc2tog) 5 times, dc5. (30)
Rnd 17 (Dc3, dc2tog) 6 times. (24)
Rnd 18 Dc6, (dc1, dc2tog)
6 times. (18)
Change to *Dark*.
Rnds 19–21 Dc. (3 rnds)
Rnd 22 (Dc2tog) 9 times. (9)

Ears *(make two)*
Work as standard in Medium until Rnd 5. (36)
Fold circle in half RS out and dc edge using *Light*.

Legs *(make four)*
Work as standard in Medium.

Making Up
See the Stuffing and Sewing and Adding Face Details sections.

Notes
Koalas do not have tails.
You can leave out the *Light* edgings on the ears if you don't have the necessary yarn – they are a bit of an indulgence!

Douglas

The Highland Cow

Douglas is a family bull with a heart even bigger than his massive head. He has a tendency towards being very tidy and, when left alone, loves nothing more than dusting around the house in his brightly coloured pants. He has an insatiable appetite, but is quite a health-conscious soul who has made a habit of reading the nutritional information on all the food in the supermarket. Endlessly well intentioned, but occasionally blinded by hunger, he has been known (more than once) to land himself short of a sandwich and white-knuckle-grasping the wrong end of a stick.

You will need

Main colour: Medium
Colour two: Light
Colour three: Dark
See also: You Will Need list in Yarns and Other Materials section and Abbreviations.

Body
Work as standard in *Medium*.

Head
Work as standard in *Medium* until:
Rnd 6 (Dc5, dc2 into next st) 6 times. (42)
Rnds 7–11 Dc.
Rnd 12 (Dc5, dc2tog) 6 times. (36)
Rnd 13 Dc.

Rnd 14 (Dc4, dc2tog) 3 times, dc18. (33)
Rnd 15 (Dc3, dc2tog) 3 times, dc18. (30)
Rnd 16 Dc.
Rnd 17 (Dc3, dc2tog) 6 times. (24)
Change to *Light*.
Rnd 18 (Dc3, dc2 into next st) 6 times. (30)
Rnds 19–21 Dc. (3 rnds)
Rnd 22 (Dc3, dc2tog) 6 times. (24)
Rnd 23 (Dc2, dc2tog) 6 times. (18)
Rnd 24 (Dc1, dc2tog) 6 times. (12)
Stuff head and close by sewing the stitches in a horizontal line (not gathering).

Ears *(make two)*
Working in *Medium*, begin by dc6 into ring.
Rnd 1 (Dc2 into next st) 6 times. (12)
Rnds 2–6 Dc. (5 rnds)
Rnd 7 (Dc2tog) 6 times (6).

Legs *(make four)*
Work as standard in *Dark* and change to *Medium* at Rnd 6.

Tail
Working in *Medium* and using four strands of the yarn held together, ch12 big sts. Attach three ch12 hair loops to end in Medium.

Top knot
Work a fringe between the ears in Medium with two rows of ch10 hair loops.

Horns *(make two)*
Working in *Light* in free-form style without rounds: ch10, join into circle, dc12, dc2tog, dc12, dc2tog, dc12, dc2tog, dc10, dc2tog,

dc10, dc2tog to a point.

Making up
See the Stuffing and Sewing and Adding Face Details sections.

Notes
Stuff horns before attaching and sew into position before adding top knot.

Laurence

The Tiger

Laurence is a foodie who is utterly convinced that he is fluent in
every language, but in reality speaks only a few quite badly.
Chivalrous to the extreme, he has missed many a train by carrying
bags up and down stairs for tigresses in distress, and is secretly
shivering when socializing with female friends. Perhaps chivalry
goes hand in hand with romance, for this tiger wines and dines in
style. He'll happily spend all day making pasta, slow-roasting lamb
and hand-rolling sushi, only to spend all night eating and whispering
sweet nonsensical nothings to one very lucky lady.

You will need

Main colour: Dark
Colour two: Medium
Colour three: Light (scrap)
See also: You Will Need list in Yarns and Other Materials section
and Abbreviations.

Body
Work as standard, beginning in *Dark* and working two-round stripes
with Medium throughout (the dc6 into ring and Rnd 1 form the first
stripe).

Head
Work as standard in *Dark* and working stripes as body until:
Rnd 6 (Dc5, dc2 into next st) 6 times. (42)
Rnds 7–11 Dc. (5 rnds)

Rnd 12 Dc10, dc2tog, (dc5, dc2tog) 3 times, dc9. (38)
Rnd 13 Dc14, dc2tog, dc6, dc2tog, dc14. (36)
Rnd 14 (Dc4, dc2tog) 6 times. (30)
Rnd 15 (Dc3, dc2tog) 6 times. (24)
Rnd 16 Dc9, dc2tog, dc2, dc2tog, dc9. (22)
Rnd 17 Dc7, dc2tog, dc2, dc2tog, dc9. (20)
Change to *Light*.
Rnds 18–19 Dc. (2 rnds)
Rnd 20 (Dc2tog) 10 times. (10)
Rnd 21 (Dc2tog) 5 times. (5)

Ears *(make two)*
Working in Medium, begin by dc6 into ring.
Rnd 1 (Dc2 into next st) 6 times. (12)
Rnds 2–4 Dc. (3 rnds)
Change to *Dark*.
Rnd 5 Dc.
Rnd 6 (Dc2tog) 6 times. (6)

Legs *(make four)*
Work as standard using *Dark* until Rnd 3 and then continue in two-round stripe pattern with Medium.

Tail
Working in *Dark*, begin by dc6 into ring.
Rnds 1–6 Dc.
Change to Medium and continue in two-round stripes to end of Rnd 26.

Making Up
See the Stuffing and Sewing and Adding Face Details sections.

Notes

Sew on the ears *Dark* part downwards onto the *Dark* ring on the back of the head.

Chardonnay

The Palomino Pony

Chardonnay is a glitter girl whose sharp business sense hides behind her white shoes and fake tan. As the owner of a luxury dog spa where rich and famous pooches come to get pampered, she is certainly used to being her own boss. It's all diamantés on toenails, sparkly suede collars and hand-knitted cashmere hoodies for these seriously indulged pets and the lady who makes it all happen. She has been online dating for the last two years and is tiring of someone else picking up the bill, especially as she's never yet found conversation to match the quality of the caviar.

You will need

Main colour: Medium
Colour two: Light
See also: You Will Need list in Yarns and Other Materials section
and Abbreviations.

Body
Work as standard in Medium.

Head
Work as standard in Medium until:
Rnd 6 (Dc5, dc2 into next st) 6 times. (42)
Rnds 7–12 Dc. (6 rnds)
Rnd 13 (Dc5, dc2tog) 6 times. (36)
Rnd 14 (Dc1, dc2tog) 12 times. (24)
Rnd 15 (Dc2, dc2tog) 6 times. (18)
Rnds 16 (Dc2, dc2 into next st) 6 times. (24)
Rnds 17–23 Dc. (7 rnds)

Rnd 24 (Dc2, dc2tog) 6 times. (18)
Rnd 25 (Dc1, dc2tog) 6 times. (12)

Ears *(make two)*
Working in Medium, begin by dc6 into ring.
Rnd 1 (Dc2 into next st) 6 times. (12)
Rnd 2 (Dc1, dc2 into next st) 6 times. (18)
Rnds 3–4 Dc. (2 rnds)
Rnd 5 (Dc1, dc2tog) 6 times. (12)
Rnd 6 Dc.
Rnd 7 (Dc2tog) 6 times. (6)
Rnd 8 (Dc2tog) 3 times. (3)

Legs *(make four)*
Work as standard in *Light*, changing to Medium at Rnd 9.

Tail
Ch30 loops in *Light* around one stitch.

Mane
Working in *Light*, work a mane up the back of the head with ch12 loops. Add more loops between the ears to create a fringe.

Making Up
See the Stuffing and Sewing and Adding Face Details sections.

Claudia

The Saddleback Pig

Claudia is a koumponophobic. Her irrational fear of buttons has set her back a few times in her life. She now works in HR by day and is planning her wedding by night. She has been engaged for just over a year and the big day is approaching at speed. Determined for everything to be perfectly unique, she has drawn the invites, sewn her bridesmaids' dresses, and plans to bake the favours. Claudia and her husband-to-be are childhood sweethearts and she knows that the day she says 'I do' will be the best day of her life. Needless to say, her dress fastens with a hidden zip.

You will need

Main colour: Dark
Colour two: Light
See also: You Will Need list in Yarns and Other Materials section and Abbreviations.

Body
Work as standard in *Dark*, changing to *Light* in middle of Rnd 19.

Head
In *Dark* work as standard until:
Rnd 6 (Dc5, dc2 into next st) 6 times. (42)
Rnds 7–11 Dc. (5 rnds)
Rnd 12 (Dc5, dc2tog) 6 times. (36)
Rnd 13 Dc.
Rnd 14 (Dc4, dc2tog) 3 times, dc18. (33)

Rnd 15 (Dc3, dc2tog) 3 times, dc18. (30)
Rnd 16 Dc.
Rnd 17 (Dc3, dc2tog) 6 times. (24)
Rnd 18 Dc12, (dc1, dc2tog) 4 times. (20)
Rnd 19 (Dc2, dc2tog) 5 times. (15)
Rnds 20–21 Dc. (2 rnds)
Rnd 22 (Dc1, dc2tog) 5 times. (10)
Rnd 23 (Dc2tog) 5 times. (5)

Ears *(make two)*
Work as standard in *Dark* until Rnd 5. (36)

Legs *(make four)*
Work as standard, making two in *Light* and two in *Dark*.

Tail
Working in *Dark*, ch10, then turn and work dc2 into every stitch back along. (20)

Making Up
See the Stuffing and Sewing and Adding Face Details sections.

Notes
To finish the ears, fold the circles in half RS out and dc halfway around the semi-circle before opening this up and sewing into position with the points forwards.
Add the nostrils in *Light*.

Alice

The Zebra

Alice is one of those best kinds of friends. She leads a staunchly independent life working hard, and when she's not knee-deep designing logos she's chasing the party around the world with an overloaded suitcase that doesn't quite close. While she is distracted by taste-testing her way across the finest delis in London, or planning her annual mane trim, you'll never hear a word out of her. But with this zebra you need never worry if the phone doesn't ring; the moment your lives collide again it will be just like the last time you met.

You will need

> Main colour: Dark
> Colour two: Light
> See also: <u>You Will Need</u> list in <u>Yarns and Other Materials</u> section
>   and <u>Abbreviations</u>.

Body
Work as <u>standard</u>, beginning in *Dark* and working two-round stripes with *Light* throughout (the dc6 into ring and Rnd 1 form the first stripe).

Head
Work as <u>standard</u>, beginning in *Light* and working two-round stripes with *Dark* until:
Rnd 6 (Dc5, dc2 into next st) 6 times. (42)
Rnds 7–12 Dc. (6 rnds)

Rnd 13 (Dc5, dc2tog) 6 times. (36)
Rnd 14 (Dc1, dc2tog) 12 times. (24)
Rnd 15 (Dc2, dc2tog) 6 times. (18)
Rnd 16 (Dc2, dc2 into next st) 6 times. (24)
Rnds 17–23 Dc. (7 rnds)
Continue in *Dark* to end:
Rnd 24 (Dc2, dc2tog) 6 times. (18)
Rnd 25 (Dc1, dc2tog) 6 times. (12)

Ears *(make two)*

Working in *Light*, begin by dc6 into ring.
Rnd 1 (Dc2 into next st) 6 times. (12)
Rnd 2 (Dc1, dc2 into next st) 6 times. (18)
Rnds 3–4 Dc. (2 rnds)
Rnd 5 (Dc1, dc2tog) 6 times. (12)
Rnd 6 Dc.
Rnd 7 (Dc2tog) 6 times. (6)
Rnd 8 (Dc2tog) 3 times. (3)

Legs *(make four)*

Work as <u>standard</u> but with Rnds 1–8 in *Dark*, then return to the striped pattern.

Tail

Working in *Light* and using four strands of the yarn held together, ch8 big sts. Attach three ch15 loops to the end in *Dark*.

Mane

Working in *Dark*, work a mane up the back of the head with ch12 loops. Add more loops between the ears to create a fringe.

Making Up

See the <u>Stuffing and Sewing</u> and <u>Adding Face Details</u> sections.

Audrey

The Nanny Goat

Audrey is a sharp-witted old goat with a penchant for sarcasm. She is a bit of a prankster and will take a schoolboy trick further than any eleven-year-old kid would dare. She takes all her hot drinks black and bitter, and saves up her annual dairy quota to be redeemed in one big cream liqueur binge in the days surrounding Christmas. Children have always found her a bit scary, as it's impossible to judge whether she's being serious or whether she's just got hold of your leg and is dragging you down the river towards a tasty-looking piece of foliage.

You will need

Main colour: Medium
Colour two: Light
See also: You Will Needl ist in Yarns and Other Materials section and Abbreviations.

Body
Work as standard in Medium.

Head
Work as standard in Medium until:
Rnd 6 (Dc5, dc2 into next st) 6 times. (42)
Rnds 7–12 Dc. (6 rnds)
Rnd 13 (Dc5, dc2tog) 6 times. (36)
Rnd 14 (Dc1, dc2tog) 12 times. (24)
Rnd 15 Dc6, (dc1, dc2tog) 6 times. (18)

Rnds 16–18 Dc. (3 rnds)
Change to *Light*.
Rnds 19–21 Dc. (3 rnds)
Rnd 22 (Dc2tog) 9 times. (9)

Beard
In *Light*, work three ch10 loops under the chin around one stitch.

Ears *(make two)*
Working in Medium, ch10 and sl st to join into circle.
Rnds 1–4 Dc. (4 rnds)
Rnd 5 (Dc4, dc2 into next st) twice. (12)
Rnd 6 Dc.
Rnd 7 (Dc5, dc2 into next st) twice. (14)
Rnds 8–10 Dc. (3 rnds)
Rnd 11 (Dc5, dc2tog) twice. (12)
Rnd 12 (Dc4, dc2tog) twice. (10)
Rnd 13 (Dc3, dc2tog) twice. (8)
Rnd 14 (Dc2, dc2tog) twice. (6)
Rnd 15 Dc.
Rnd 16 (Dc2tog) 3 times. (3)
Rnd 17 Dc3tog.

Legs *(make four)*
Work as standard in *Light*, changing to Medium at Rnd 12.

Tail
Working in Medium and using four strands of the yarn held together, ch8 big sts then work three ch8 loops on the end.

Horns *(make two)*
Working in *Light* in free-form style: ch8 and join into a circle, dc30, dc2tog, dc5, dc2tog, (dc1, dc2tog) twice, dc4, dc2tog to a point.

Making Up

See the Stuffing and Sewing and Adding Face Details sections.

level 3

Level 3 animals introduce some more complex techniques, so it is advisable to have made at least one Level 1 and one Level 2 animal before embarking on these. Many of these patterns require the use of irregular shade changing: rather than cutting the yarn, you run it along the WS of the fabric, being careful not to pull the changes too tight to avoid puckering the fabric. Some of these patterns also include fur stitch; this involves only one extra step to the standard double crochet stitch, so don't be intimidated by its appearance. Occasionally you will need to use the technique of traversing the fabric using slip stitch (see the Technicals section) and working end-of-row stitches through the fabric.

Clarence

The Bat

Clarence spends most of his waking hours in a hard hat. As a structural engineer he thoroughly enjoys his job hanging around under bridges drinking milky tea and mocking the truck driver who did not know that his trailer was higher than the clearance. He is a collector of expensive Persian rugs, which he uses to make his inadequately heated house a bit more comfortable. You can see your breath in every room with the exception of the large and very ugly conservatory where Clarence sensitively nurses hundreds of plants. When Clarence is not taking them to the local railway museum, his young nephews love nothing more than playing with their favourite uncle's Venus flytraps.

You will need

Main colour: Medium
Colour two: Dark
See also: You Will Need list in Yarns and Other Materials section and Abbreviations.

Body
Work as standard in Medium.

Head
Work as standard in Medium until:
Rnd 6 (Dc5, dc2 into next st) 6 times. (42)
Rnds 7–11 Dc. (5 rnds)
Rnd 12 (Dc5, dc2tog) 6 times. (36)

Rnd 13 Dc.
Rnd 14 (Dc4, dc2tog) 3 times, dc18. (33)
Rnd 15 (Dc3, dc2tog) 3 times, dc18. (30)
Rnd 16 Dc.
Rnd 17 (Dc3, dc2tog) 6 times. (24)
Rnd 18 Dc12, (dc1, dc2tog)
4 times. (20)
Rnd 19 (Dc2, dc2tog) 5 times. (15)
Rnd 20 (Dc2tog) 7 times, dc1. (8)
Rnd 21 (Dc2tog) 4 times. (4)

Ears *(make two)*
Working in Medium, ch 20 and sl st to join into circle.
Rnd 1 (Dc8, dc2tog) twice. (18)
Rnd 2 Dc.
Rnd 3 (Dc7, dc2tog) twice. (16)
Rnds 4–7 Dc. (4 rnds)
Rnd 8 (Dc6, dc2tog) twice. (14)
Rnd 9 Dc.
Rnd 10 (Dc5, dc2tog) twice. (12)
Rnd 11 (Dc2, dc2tog) 3 times. (9)
Rnd 12 (Dc1, dc2tog) 3 times. (6)
Rnd 13 Dc.
Rnd 14 (Dc2tog) 3 times. (3)

Legs *(make four)*
Make two in *Medium* as standard, then work two as standard in *Medium* until:
Rnd 7 (Dc1, dc2tog) 6 times. (12)
Rnd 8 (Dc4, dc2tog) twice. (10)
Rnds 9–33 Dc. (25 rnds)

Wings (repeat on both sides)

Working in *Dark*, sew arms in place, then dc into a central st of armpit, ch3 and dc to top of body. Dc3 sts into space between the chain and body. Work these sts backwards and forwards in dc, picking up 1 st per row from body or arm before turning until you reach the bottom of the body. Continue to work but turning back 3 sts from the end to shape the wing to a central point. Finish by tidying up the wing by placing a dc into every st along the edge.

Making Up
See the Stuffing and Sewing and Adding Face Details sections.

Notes
Sew the ears in place high up on the back of the head by oversewing around the bottom third of the ear.

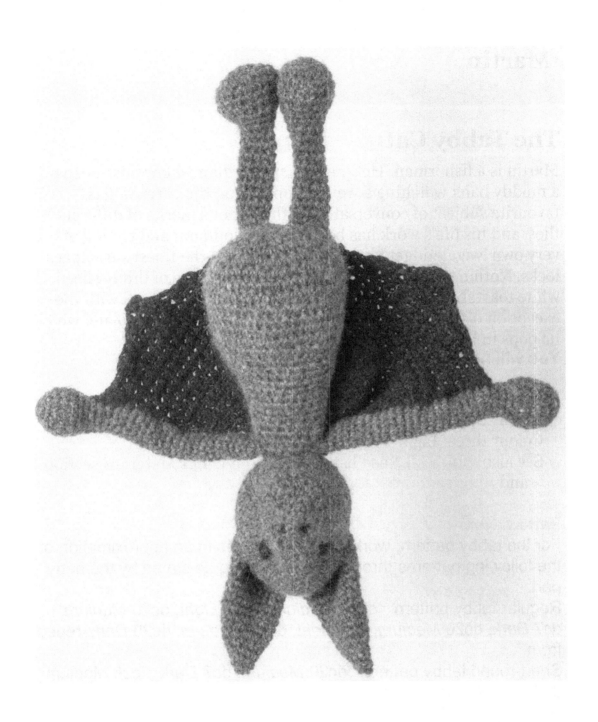

Martin

The Tabby Cat

Martin is a fisherman. He's never happier than when waist-deep off a muddy bank watching a weight bobbing on the current. His favourite subject of conversation is the various merits of different flies, and his life's work has been the development and testing of his very own 'wiggletidger', hand-crocheted from the finest suri alpaca locks. Nothing passes his lips unless it's on a piece of thinly sliced white toast; breakfast, lunch or tea. That is, every morsel with the exception of his nightly square of 97 per cent cocoa chocolate, which he pops in his mouth and lets melt slowly in its own time.

You will need

Main colour: Medium
Colour two: Dark
Colour three: Light
See also: You Will Need list in Yarns and Other Materials section
  and Abbreviations

Pattern Note
For the tabby pattern, work the three shades in an approximation of the following patterns throughout all shaping as stated by the body part:
Regular tabby pattern: *dc20 *Medium*, dc20 *Light*, dc20 *Medium*, dc7 *Dark*, dc20 *Medium*, dc7 *Light*, dc20 *Medium*, dc20 *Dark*, repeat from *.
Short-round tabby pattern: *dc20 *Medium*, dc7 *Dark*, dc20 Medium, dc7 *Light*, repeat from *.

Body

Work as standardi n regular tabby pattern.

Head
Work as standard in regular tabby pattern until:
Rnd 6 (Dc5, dc2 into next st) 6 times. (42)
Rnds 7–11 Dc. (5 rnds)
Rnd 12 (Dc5, dc2tog) 6 times. (36)
Rnd 13 (Dc4, dc2tog) 6 times. (30)
Rnd 14 (Dc3, dc2tog) 6 times. (24)
Rnd 15 Dc.
Rnd 16 (Dc1, dc2tog) 8 times. (16)
Rnd 17 Dc.
Rnd 18 (Dc2, dc2tog) 4 times. (12)
Change to *Light* only.
Rnd 19 (Dc2tog) 6 times. (6)
Rnd 20 (Dc2tog) 3 times. (3)

Ears *(make two)*
Make two in short-round tabby pattern: *dc20 Medium, dc7 *Dark*,
dc20 Medium, dc7 *Light*, repeat from *.
Ch10 and sl st to join into circle.
Rnd 1 Dc.
Rnd 2 (Dc2 into next st) 10 times. (20)
Rnds 3–4 Dc. (2 rnds)
Rnd 5 (Dc8, dc2tog) twice. (18)
Rnd 6 (Dc7, dc2tog) twice. (16)
Rnd 7 Dc.
Rnd 8 (Dc6, dc2tog) twice. (14)
Rnd 9 (Dc5, dc2tog) twice. (12)
Rnd 10 (Dc4, dc2tog) twice. (10)
Rnd 11 (Dc3, dc2tog) twice. (8)
Rnd 12 (Dc2, dc2tog) twice. (6)
Rnd 13 (Dc1, dc2tog) twice. (4)

Rnd 14 Dc4tog.

Legs *(make four)*
Work as <u>standard</u> in short-round tabby pattern.

Tail
Working in short-round tabby pattern, begin by dc6 into ring.
Rnds 1–26 Dc.

Making Up
See the <u>Stuffing and Sewing</u> and <u>Adding Face Details</u> sections.

Notes
Sew the ears in place on the back of the head by oversewing around the bottom third of the ear, ensuring you can see them from the front.

Sarah

The Friesian Cow

Sarah works part-time in an ice-cream factory, stirring and whirling the finest locally sourced organic ingredients into the most mouth-watering pots of frozen yumminess. When she's not developing new recipes she is standing on the touchline cheering on any one of her four teenage boys, who all excel on the sports field. As a result she runs two toploading washing machines almost around the clock and knows exactly the correct temperature, soak time and spin cycle to select to guarantee perfect whites despite grass, mud and raspberry ripple.

You will need

Main colour: Dark
Colour two: Light
See also: You Will Need list in Yarns and Other Materials section
and Abbreviations.

Body
Work as standard in *Dark*, changing to *Light* in the middle of Rnd 14 and then back to *Dark* in the middle of Rnd 22.

Head
Work as standard in *Dark* until:
Rnd 6 (Dc5, dc2 into next st)
6 times. (42)
Rnds 7–11 Dc. (5 rnds)

Rnd 12 (Dc5, dc2tog) 4 times *Dark*, dc7 *Light*, (dc5, dc2tog) *Dark*. (37)

Rnd 13 Dc21, dc2tog *Dark*, dc9 *Light*, dc5 *Dark*. (36)

Rnd 14 Dc23, dc2tog in *Dark*, dc2 *Light*, dc2tog, dc5, dc2tog *Dark*. (33)

Rnd 15 Dc21, dc2tog, dc2 *Dark*, dc2 *Light*, dc2tog, dc4 *Dark*. (31)

Rnd 16 Dc2tog, dc21 *Dark*, dc5 *Light*, dc3 *Dark*. (30)

Rnd 17 (Dc3, dc2tog) 4 times, dc3 *Dark*, dc2tog, dc1 *Light*, dc2, dc2tog *Dark*. (24)

Rnd 18 (Dc3, dc2 into next st) 4 times, dc3 *Dark*, dc2 into next st *Light*, dc3, dc2 into next st *Dark*. (30)

Rnd 19 Dc10 *Dark*, dc20 *Light*. (30)
Continue to end in *Light* only.

Rnds 20–21 Dc. (2 rnds)

Rnd 22 (Dc3, dc2tog) 6 times. (24)

Rnd 23 (Dc2, dc2tog) 6 times. (18)

Rnd 24 (Dc1, dc2tog) 6 times. (12)
Stuff head and close by sewing the stitches in a horizontal line (not gathering).

Ears *(make two)*
Working in *Dark*, begin by dc6 into ring.

Rnd 1 (Dc2 into next st) 6 times. (12)

Rnds 2–6 Dc. (5 rnds)

Rnd 7 (Dc2tog) 6 times. (6)

LEGS *(make four)*
Work as standard in *Dark*, changing to *Light* at Rnd 6.

Tail
Working in *Light* and using four strands of the yarn held together, ch12 big sts. Work three ch12 loops to end in *Dark*.

Making Up
See the Stuffing and Sewing and Adding Face Details sections.

Timmy

The Jack Russell Dog

Timmy is a mischievous pup who schedules his days so he's only ever an hour away from his next meal. Despite being good at swimming, climbing, map reading and every other skill you might need to be a good adventurer, he never gets very far due to his habit of eating all of the picnic on the way there. He has broken the same leg three times, dreams of pirates, smugglers and kidnappers, and is particularly partial to a pint of ginger beer, a pork pie and a pickled onion sandwich.

You will need

Main colour: Light
Colour two: Dark
See also: You Will Need list in Yarns and Other Materials section and Abbreviations.

Body
Work as standard in *Dark*, changing to *Light* in the middle of Rnd 14.

Head
Work as standard in *Light* until:
Rnd 6 (Dc5, dc2 into next st) 6 times. (42)
Rnd 7 Dc.
Rnd 8 Dc8 *Dark*, dc10 *Light*, dc24 *Dark*.
Rnd 9 Dc10 *Dark*, dc6 *Light*, dc26 *Dark*.
Rnd 10 Dc12 *Dark*, dc2 *Light*, dc28 *Dark*.
Rnd 11 Dc13 *Dark*, dc1 *Light*, dc28 *Dark*.

Continue to end in *Dark* only.
Rnd 12 Dc.
Rnd 13 (Dc5, dc2tog) 6 times. (36)
Rnd 14 (Dc4, dc2tog) 6 times. (30)
Rnd 15 (Dc1, dc2tog) 10 times. (20)
Change to *Light*.
Rnd 16 (Dc2tog, dc1, dc2tog) 4 times. (12)
Rnd 17 (Dc2, dc2tog) 3 times. (9)
Rnd 18 (Dc2tog) 4 times, dc1. (5)
Rnd 19 (Dc2tog) twice, dc1. (3)

Ears *(make two)*
Working in *Dark*, work as standard up to Rnd 3. (24)
Rnd 4 Dc.
Rnd 5 (Dc2, dc2tog) 6 times. (18)
Rnds 6–8 Dc. (3 rnds)
Rnd 9 (Dc1, dc2tog) 6 times. (12)
Rnds 10–11 Dc. (2 rnds)
Rnd 12 (Dc2tog) 6 times. (6)
Rnd 13 Dc.
Rnd 14 (Dc2tog) 3 times. (3)

Legs *(make four)*
Work as standard in *Light*.

Tail
Working in *Light*, begin by ch8 and sl st to join into circle.
Rnd 1 Dc.
Rnd 2 Dc6, dc2tog. (7)
Rnd 3 Dc5, dc2tog. (6)
Rnd 4 Dc4, dc2tog. (5)
Rnd 5 Dc3, dc2tog. (4)
Rnd 6 (Dc2tog) twice. (2)

Making Up
See the Stuffing and Sewing and Adding Face Details sections.

Notes
Stuff the tail firmly.
Finish the ears by pinching and sewing into place on the back of the head. Create character by tacking one down while leaving one upright.

Caitlin

The Giraffe

Caitlin is one nosy giraffe. Life as a home science teacher just doesn't give her enough to talk about, but thankfully her active role as WI chairperson gives her the perfect excuse to know everyone else's business. That said, it's not as if she needs much gossip to go on; her skills at telling a tale mean she can spin richly elaborate scenarios from a tiny morsel of information. If you're ever wondering about the cousin of your neighbour's boyfriend's cat (or the shade of his pants), Caitlin is the one to ask.

You will need

>Main colour: Light
>Colour two: Medium
>Colour three: Dark
>See also: You Will Need list in Yarns and Other Materials section
>and Abbreviations.

Body
Work as standard beginning in *Light* and working patches of Medium comprised of approximately 9 sts at random throughout until:
Rnd 21 (Dc2, dc2tog) 6 times. (24)
Rnds 22–29 Dc. (8 rnds)
Rnd 30 (Dc2, dc2tog) 6 times. (18)
Rnds 31–33 Dc. (3 rnds)
Rnd 34 (Dc1, dc2tog) 6 times. (12)
Rnds 35–37 Dc. (3 rnds)
Rnd 38 (Dc2tog) 6 times. (6)

Head
Work as standard in *Light* until:
Rnd 6 (Dc5, dc2 into next st) 6 times. (42)
Rnds 7–11 Dc. (5 rnds)
Rnd 12 (Dc5, dc2tog) 6 times. (36)
Rnd 13 (Dc4, dc2tog) 6 times. (30)
Rnd 14 (Dc3, dc2tog) 6 times. (24)
Change to Medium.
Rnd 15 Dc12, (dc1, dc2tog) 4 times. (20)
Rnds 16–19 Dc. (5 rnds)
Rnd 20 (Dc2, dc2tog) 5 times. (15)
Rnd 21 (Dc1, dc2tog) 5 times. (10)
Rnd 22 (Dc2tog) 5 times. (5)

Ears *(make two)*
Working in *Light*, begin by ch9 and sl st to join into circle.
Rnds 1–5 Dc. (5 rnds)
Rnd 6 (Dc1, dc2tog) 3 times. (6)
Rnd 7 (Dc2tog) 3 times. (3)

Legs *(make four)*
Work as standard in *Dark*, changing to *Light* at Rnd 6 and continuing length by 6 rnds (to Rnd 30).

Tail
Working in *Light* and using four strands of yarn held together, ch10 big sts. Work five ch12 loops to end in *Dark*.

Ossicones *(horns)*
Working in *Dark*, begin by dc8 into ring. Change to Medium.
Rnd 1 (Dc2tog) 4 times. (4)
Rnds 2–5 Dc. (4 rnds)

Making Up
See the Stuffing and Sewing and Adding Face Details sections.

Esme

The Fox

Esme is a crafty fox. She makes her own greetings cards, sews, knits and crochets; she'll turn her hand to pretty much anything that involves needles or PVA glue. She has seven children who have an extensive dressing-up box and are always winning school costume competitions. Whether it's for the Nativity, Easter Parade or Halloween, this vixen knows exactly how to throw together the perfect outfit. When she's not threading elastic through headdresses or gluing beads onto shoes she sells her six-shade intarsia tea cosies through an online marketplace.

You will need

Main colour: Dark
Colour two: Light
See also: You Will Need list in Yarns and Other Materials section
and Abbreviations.

Body
Work as standard in *Dark*.

Head
Work as standard in *Dark* until:
Rnd 6 (Dc5, dc2 into next st) 6 times. (42)
Rnds 7–9 Dc. (3 rnds)
Rnds 10–11 Dc18 *Light*, dc24 *Dark*.
Rnd 12 Dc1 *Dark*, dc16 *Light*, (dc2, dc2tog) 6 times, dc1 *Dark*. (36)
Rnd 13 Dc3 *Dark*, dc13 *Light*, dc20 *Dark*.

Rnd 14 Dc3, dc2tog *Dark*, (dc3, dc2tog) twice *Light*, (dc3, dc2tog) 3 times *Dark*. (30)

Rnd 15 Dc5 *Dark*, dc7 *Light*, dc18 *Dark*.

Rnd 16 Dc2, dc2tog, dc2 *Dark*, dc2tog, dc2, dc2tog *Light*, (dc4, dc2tog) 3 times *Dark*. (24)

Rnd 17 Dc2, dc2tog, dc2 *Dark*, dc2tog *Light*, (dc2, dc2tog) 4 times *Dark*. (18)

Continue to end in *Dark* only.

Rnd 18 (Dc1, dc2tog) 6 times. (12)

Rnd 19 Dc.

Rnd 20 (Dc2, dc2tog) 3 times. (9)

Rnd 21 (Dc3tog) 3 times. (3)

Ears *(make two)*
Working in *Dark*, ch12 and sl st to join into circle.

Rnds 1–2 Dc. (2 rnds)

Rnd 3 (Dc4, dc2tog) twice. (10)

Rnd 4 (Dc3, dc2tog) twice. (8)

Rnd 5 (Dc2, dc2tog) twice. (6)

Rnd 6 (Dc1, dc2tog) twice. (4)

Rnd 7 Dc.

Rnd 8 (Dc2tog) twice. (2)

Legs *(make four)*
Work as standard in *Dark*.

Tail
Working in *Dark*, ch8 and sl st to join into circle.

Rnds 1–4 Dc. (4 rnds)

Rnd 5 (Dc3, dc2 into next st) twice. (10)

Rnds 6–9 Dc. (4 rnds)

Rnd 10 (Dc4, dc2 into next st) twice. (12)

Rnds 11–13 Dc. (3 rnds)

Rnd 14 (Dc2, dc2 into next st) 4 times. (16)
Change to *Light*.
Rnd 15 (Dc3, dc2 into next st) 4 times. (20)
Rnds 16–19 Dc. (4 rnds)
Rnd 20 (Dc3, dc2tog) 4 times. (16)
Rnd 21 (Dc2, dc2tog) 4 times. (12)
Rnd 22 (Dc2tog) 6 times. (6)
Rnd 23 (Dc2tog) 3 times. (3)

Making Up
See the Stuffing and Sewing and Adding Face Details sections.

Notes
Stuff the end of the tail only. Dc the other end flat.

Blake

The Orang-utan

Blake is a self-employed tree surgeon. He has set his pace of life to guarantee that he has plenty of time to smell the roses and steam-mop his slate bathroom floors. This orang-utan is a domesticated ape; he cleans, he bakes, and he spends three days a week changing nappies and making purée for his one-year-old twin daughters. Some say he is something of a modern philosopher, pulling insight and truth from his hairy navel as casually as others blow their noses. So when he's not swinging from the treetops or wearing his apron, he's keeping a journal that would be well worth a read.

You will need

Main colour: Dark
Colour two: Light
See also: <u>You Will Need</u> list in <u>Yarns and Other Materials</u> section and <u>Abbreviations</u>.

Pattern Note
Work <u>fur stitch</u> when instructed every 3rd st on odd rows and every 4th st on even rows. Fur stitch is worked on the WS so Blake is effectively inside out. You can pull these stitches through to the RS at the end if desired.

Body
Work as <u>standard</u> in *Dark* using fur stitch.

Head
Work as standard in *Dark* using fur stitch as above until:
Rnd 6 (Dc5, dc2 into next st) 6 times. (42)
Rnds 7–11 Dc. (5 rnds)
Rnd 12 (Dc5, dc2tog) 6 times. (36)
Rnd 13 Dc.
Rnd 14 (Dc4, dc2tog) 3 times, dc18. (33)
Rnd 15 (Dc3, dc2tog) 3 times, dc18. (30)
At this point stop working in fur stitch for remainder.
Rnd 16 Dc.
Rnd 17 (Dc3, dc2tog) 6 times. (24)
Rnd 18 Dc12, (dc1, dc2tog) 4 times. (20)
Rnd 19 (Dc2, dc2tog) 5 times. (15)
Rnd 20 (Dc2tog) 7 times, dc1. (8)

Muzzle
Work as standard in *Light* without fur stitch until:
Rnd 3 (Dc2, dc2 into next st) 6 times. (24)
Rnds 4–6 Dc. (3 rnds).

Ears *(make two)*
Working in *Dark* without fur stitch, begin by dc4 into ring.
Rnd 1 (Dc2 into next st) 4 times. (8)
Rnds 2–3 Dc. (2 rnds)
Rnd 4 (Dc2tog) 4 times. (4)

Legs *(make four)*
Work two as standard, beginning in *Light* and without fur stitch.
Change to *Dark* at Rnd 2 and work in fur stitch.
Work two as above but continue length by 6 rnds (to Rnd 30) (these legs become the 'arms').

Eye patches *(make two)*

Working in *Light* without fur stitch, begin by dc6 into ring.
Rnd 1 (Dc2 into next st) 6 times. (12)

Making Up
See the Stuffing and Sewing and Adding Face Details sections.

Notes
Stuff the muzzle and sew it into place on the non-fur-stitch section of the head. After assembling, cut all of the loops to create the fur effect.

Siegfried

The Monkey

No one really knows where in the world Siegfried is from, as he boasts a phenomenally complex accent that takes a lot of concentration to decipher, even before he's finished his first gin and tonic of the day. Whatever he may have been before, he is now a middle-aged academic monkey who has spent his life searching for someone he has never found. He has been giving up smoking 'tomorrow' for the last ten years of his life and has written a sonnet every Friday night across that same decade.

You will need

Main colour: Medium
Colour two: Dark
Colour three: Light (scrap)
See also: You Will Need list in Yarns and Other Materials section and Abbreviations.

Body
Work as standard in *Medium*.

Head
Work as standard in *Medium* until:
Rnd 6 (Dc5, dc2 into next st) 6 times. (42)
Rnds 7–11 Dc. (5 rnds)
Rnd 12 (Dc5, dc2tog) 6 times. (36)
Rnd 13–14 Work these two rnds in *Light* and fur stitch making a loop every third st then change back to *Medium* to continue:

124

Rnd 15 (Dc4, dc2tog) 3 times, dc18. (33)
Rnd 16 (Dc3, dc2tog) 3 times, dc18. (30)
Rnd 17 Dc.
Rnd 18 (Dc3, dc2tog) 6 times. (24)
Rnd 19 Dc12, (dc1, dc2tog) 4 times. (20)
Rnd 20 (Dc2, dc2tog) 5 times. (15)
Rnd 21 (Dc2tog) 7 times, dc1. (8)

Muzzle
Work as standard in *Dark* until:
Rnd 3 (Dc2, dc2 into next st) 6 times (24 sts)
Rnds 4–6 Dc (3 rnds).

Ears *(make two)*
Working in *Dark*, begin by dc4 into ring.
Rnd 1 (Dc2 into next st) 4 times. (8)
Rnd 2 (Dc2 into next st) 8 times. (16)
Rnds 3–6 Dc. (4 rnds)
Rnd 7 (Dc2tog) 8 times. (8)
Rnd 8 (Dc2tog) 4 times. (4)

Legs *(make four)*
Work two as standard in *Dark* and change to *Light* at Rnd 6.
Work two as standard with the same colour change, but continue length by 8 rnds (to Rnd 30) (these legs become the 'arms').

Tail
Working in *Medium*, begin by dc8 into ring.
Rnds 1–36 Dc.

Eye patches *(make two)*
Working in *Dark*, begin by dc6 into ring.
Rnd 1 (Dc2 into next st) 6 times. (12)

Making up
See the Stuffing and Sewing and Adding Face Details sections.

Notes
When using fur stitch your 'loops' will be on WS. Pull the loops through to the RS before cutting them and then stuffing the head. Stuff the muzzle and sew into place with the eye patches just above. Complete with the eyes and nostrils.

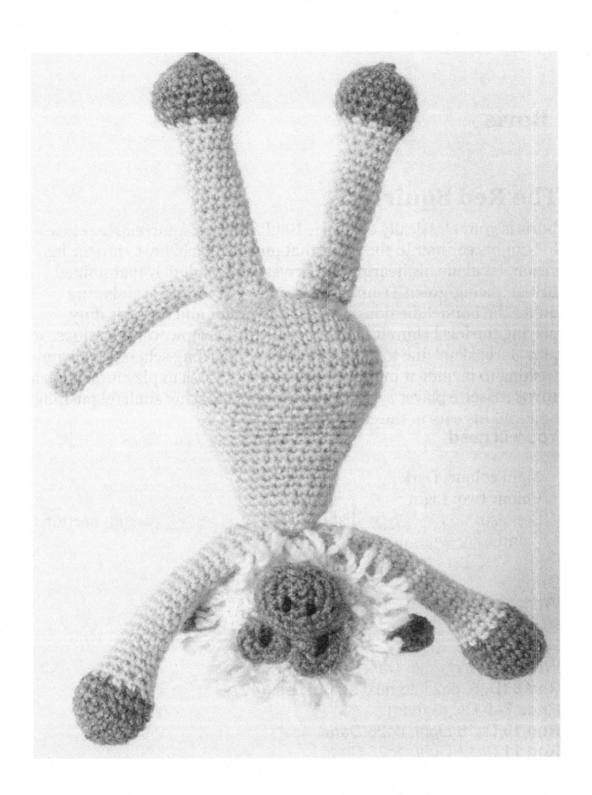

Boris

The Red Squirrel

Boris is your classically eccentric English gentlesquirrel. He refuses to trim his ear hair to the point that one day it's likely to impair his vision, let alone his hearing. He drives a meticulously maintained British racing-green Triumph Stag and, when he's not tinkering under the bonnet, he dons his best tweed suit and does his duty playing the local church's ancient pipe organ. However, he refuses to play 'Jerusalem' due to bad memories of boarding school, so anyone wishing to include it in their wedding service has to play it through a 1970s cassette player system and tolerate a rocking squirrel pushing hair into his ears in the corner.

You will need

Main colour: Dark
Colour two: Light
See also: You Will Need list in Yarns and Other Materials section and Abbreviations.

Body
Work as standard in *Dark*.

Head
Work as standard in *Dark* until:
Rnd 6 (Dc5, dc2 into next st) 6 times. (42)
Rnds 7–9 Dc. (3 rnds)
Rnd 10 Dc16 *Light*, dc26 *Dark*.
Rnd 11 Dc17 *Light*, dc25 *Dark*.

Rnd 12 Dc1 *Dark*, dc16 *Light*, (dc2, dc2tog) 6 times, dc1 *Dark*. (36)
Rnd 13 Dc2 *Dark*, dc15 *Light*, dc19 *Dark*.
Rnd 14 Dc2 *Dark*, dc2, dc2tog, dc4, dc2tog, dc3, dc2tog *Light*, (dc3, dc2tog) 3 times, dc4 *Dark*. (30)
Rnd 15 Dc3 *Dark*, dc10 *Light*, dc17 *Dark*.
Rnd 16 Dc3 *Dark*, (dc2tog, dc3) twice *Light*, (dc2tog, dc3) 3 times, dc2tog *Dark*. (24)
Rnd 17 Dc4 *Dark*, dc6 *Light*, dc14 *Dark*.
Rnd 18 Dc2, dc2tog in *Dark*, dc2, dc2tog, dc2 in *Light*, dc2tog, (dc2, dc2tog) 3 times in *Dark*. (18)
Rnd 19 Dc4 *Dark*, dc4 *Light*, dc10 *Dark*.
Continue to end in *Dark* only.
Rnd 20 (Dc2tog) 9 times. (9)
Rnd 21 (Dc2tog) 4 times, dc1. (5)

Ears *(make two)*
Work as standard in *Dark* up to Rnd 2. (18)
Rnds 3–4 Dc. (2 rnds)
Rnd 5 (Dc1, dc2tog) 6 times. (12)
Rnds 6–7 Dc. (2 rnds)
Rnd 8 (Dc2tog) 6 times. (6)
Rnd 9 (Dc2tog) 3 times. (3)
Rnd 10 Dc3tog.

Legs *(make four)*
Work as standard in *Dark*.

Tail
Work in fur stitch every 2 sts throughout. Starting in *Dark*, ch15 and sl st to join into circle.
Rnds 1–24 Dc (with loops) in *Dark*.
Rnds 25–28 Dc (with loops) in *Light*. (4 rnds)
Rnd 29 (Dc2tog) 7 times, dc1. (8)

Making Up

See the Stuffing and Sewing and Adding Face Details sections.

Notes

Stuff the tail. If desired, sew the bottom of the tail up the back by a few centimetres to ensure that it sits up behind the head.

To finish off the ears, sew three loops in *Light* into each ear.

Hamlet

The Cheetah

Hamlet is most commonly spotted reflected in your headlights at 6.30pm on your commute home from work. To say that he is addicted to cycling would not be an exaggeration. In fact, he doesn't feel normal unless he's wearing Lycra and his feet are whirring him along faster than 50 miles an hour for at least five of his waking hours every day. He is continually at risk of burning off more calories than he can consume, and so tops himself up with green power shakes and buffalo jerky. He has a complete aversion to towels but loves a long shower, so if you have the rare experience of spotting him off his wheels you can find him at the end of a line of damp paw prints.

You will need

Main colour: Medium
Colour two: Dark
Colour three: Light (scrap)
See also: You Will Need list in Yarns and Other Materials section and Abbreviations.

Body
Work as standard, beginning in Medium and working one or two stitches in *Dark* at random throughout to create spots.

Head
Work as standard in spot pattern as above until:
Rnd 6 (Dc5, dc2 into next st) 6 times. (42)

Rnds 7–11 Dc. (5 rnds)
Rnd 12 Dc10, dc2tog, (dc5, dc2tog) 3 times, dc9. (38)
Rnd 13 Dc14, dc2tog, dc6, dc2tog, dc14. (36)
Rnd 14 (Dc4, dc2tog) 6 times. (30)
Rnd 15 (Dc3, dc2tog) 6 times. (24)
Rnd 16 Dc9, dc2tog, dc2, dc2tog, dc9. (22)
Rnd 17 Dc7, dc2tog, dc2, dc2tog, dc9. (20)
Change to *Light*.
Rnds 18–19 Dc. (2 rnds)
Rnd 20 (Dc2tog) 10 times. (10)
Rnd 21 (Dc2tog) 5 times. (5)

Ears *(make two)*
Working in Medium, begin by dc6 into ring.
Rnd 1 (Dc2 into next st) 6 times. (12)
Rnds 2–4 Dc. (3 rnds)
Rnd 5 Dc.
Change to *Light*.
Rnd 6 (Dc2tog) 6 times. (6)

Legs *(make four)*
Work as <u>standard</u> in Medium plain for first 6 rnds, then continue in spot pattern as for body.

Tail
Working in *Dark*, begin by dc6 into ring.
Rnds 1–6 Dc in *Dark*. (6 rnds)
Swap to Medium and continue in spot pattern to end of Rnd 26.

Making Up
See the <u>Stuffing and Sewing</u> and <u>Adding Face Details</u> sections.

Notes

Stitch on the ears with the highlights upwards.
Stitch on the eyes and then complete the face with a stitched black border from the eyes down around the muzzle.

Francis

The Hedgehog

Francis is a petrolhead: be careful crossing the road in front of him because (as he will tell you at great length) the exhaust he fitted to his uncle's old hatchback upped the power on his wheels by 18 per cent. Nothing gets his spines tingling more than showing off his obscenely loud bass bins to his mates in the car park of the local fast-food joint. He has been dating the same young sow for five years now and thinks she might be the one to make him settle down and start developing a taste for olives, backgammon and sensibly early nights.

You will need

Main colour: Medium
Colour two: Dark
Colour three: Light
See also: You Will Need list in Yarns and Other Materials section and Abbreviations.

Body
Work as standard in Medium.

Head
Work as standard in Medium until:
Rnd 6 (Dc5, dc2 into next st) 6 times. (42)
Rnd 7 Dc.
Rnd 8 Dc8 *Light*, dc10 Medium, dc24 *Light*.
Rnd 9 Dc10 *Light*, dc6 Medium, dc26 *Light*.

Rnd 10 Dc12 *Light*, dc2 Medium, dc28 *Light*.
Rnd 11 Dc13 *Light*, dc1 Medium, dc28 *Light*.
Continue to end in *Light* only.
Rnd 12 Dc.
Rnd 13 (Dc5, dc2tog) 6 times. (36)
Rnd 14 (Dc4, dc2tog) 6 times. (30)
Rnd 15 (Dc1, dc2tog) 10 times. (20)
Rnd 16 (Dc2tog) 4 times, dc12. (16)
Rnds 17–19 Dc. (3 rnds)
Rnd 20 (Dc2, dc2tog) 4 times. (12)
Rnd 21 (Dc2, dc2tog) 3 times. (9)
Rnd 22 (Dc2tog) 4 times, dc1. (5)

Ears *(make two)*
Working in Medium, begin by dc6 into ring.
Rnd 1 (Dc2 into next st) 6times. (12)
Rnds 2–4 Dc. (3 rnds)
Rnd 5 (Dc2tog) 6 times. (6)

Legs *(make four)*
Work as standard in Medium.

Spikes
Working in *Dark*, *dc into the desired spike position into the fabric around a stitch. Ch5, then work back down the chain with four sl sts to the root of the chain. Slip stitch traverse across the fabric and then repeat from *.

Making Up
See the Stuffing and Sewing and Adding Face Details sections.

Notes

Work the spikes over the whole of the head and the back covering half of the body and down to where the legs are attached.

Jessie

The Raccoon

Jessie is the managing raccoon at the local recycling centre. Obsessed by saving the planet and making this world a greener place through his job, he really wants to make a difference. He is a real dinner-party bore due to his in-depth knowledge of plastic production and the various options for reusing tyres to improve community facilities. He is surely destined for a role on the local council, where he'll be able to meticulously ponder over every seemingly insignificant waste-disposal policy and recommend and influence to his heart's content.

You will need

Main colour: Medium
Colour two: Light
Colour three: Dark
See also: You Will Need list in Yarns and Other Materials section and Abbreviations.

Body
Work as standard in Medium.

Head
Work as standard in Medium until:
Rnd 6 (Dc5, dc2 into next st) 6 times. (42)
Rnds 7–11 Dc.
Rnd 12 Dc34 Medium, dc8 *Light*.

Rnd 13 Dc4, dc2tog, dc3 *Medium*, dc2, dc2tog, dc5 *Light*, dc2tog, dc5, dc2tog, dc5, dc2tog *Medium*, dc3, dc2tog, dc3 *Light*. (36)
Rnd 14 Dc3, dc2tog, dc2 *Medium*, dc2, dc2tog, dc4 *Light*, dc2tog, dc4, dc2tog, dc4, dc2tog *Medium*, dc4, dc2tog, dc1 *Light*. (30)
Rnd 15 Dc1 *Light*, dc6 *Medium*, dc7 *Light*, dc11 *Medium*, dc5 *Light*.
Rnd 16 Dc2 *Light*, dc1, dc2tog, dc2 *Medium*, dc3 *Dark*, dc2tog, dc3 *Light*, dc2tog, dc3, dc2tog, dc1, dc2tog *Medium*, dc2tog, dc2 *Light*, dc1 *Dark*. (24)
Rnd 17 Dc2 *Dark*, dc4 *Medium*, dc6 *Dark*, dc9 *Medium*, dc3 *Dark*.
Rnd 18 Dc2 *Dark*, dc2tog, dc2 *Medium*, dc2tog, dc2, dc2tog *Dark*, dc2, dc2tog, dc2, dc2tog, dc1 *Medium*, dc1, dc2tog *Dark*. (18)
Rnd 19 Dc3 *Dark*, dc2 *Medium*, dc5 *Dark*, dc7 *Medium*, dc1 *Dark*.
Rnd 20 (Dc1, dc2tog) 3 times, dc1 *Dark*, dc2tog, (dc1, dc2tog) twice *Light*. (12)
Rnd 21 Dc *Light*.
Rnd 22 (Dc1, dc2tog) 4 times. (8)
Rnd 23 (Dc2tog) 4 times. (4)

Ears *(make two)*
Starting in *Medium*, ch15 and sl st to join into circle.
Rnds 1–4 Dc *Medium*.
Rnd 5 (Dc1, dc2tog) 5 times *Light*. (10)
Rnd 6 (Dc2tog) 5 times. (5)

Legs *(make four)*
Work as standard in *Medium*.

Tail
Work in as fur stitch every 2 sts throughout.
Working in *Light*, ch12 and sl st to join into circle.
Rnds 1–5 Dc *Light*. (5 rnds)
Rnds 6–11 Dc *Dark*. (6 rnds)
Rnds 12–16 Dc *Light*. (5 rnds

Rnds 17–21 Dc *Dark*. (5 rnds)
Rnds 22–26 Dc *Light*. (5 rnds)
Rnds 27–31 Dc *Dark*. (5 rnds)
Rnd 32 (Dc1, dc2tog) 4 times *Dark*. (8)

Making Up
See the Stuffing and Sewing and Adding Face Details sections.

Bradlee

The Grey Squirrel

Bradlee is a sports squirrel. He can turn his rippling muscles to most field sports, but lacrosse silverware fills the majority of the shelves in his trophy cabinet. He's always been in with the in-crowd and works hard to keep his body and his reputation in peak condition. Each morning he does 30 push-ups and has a swim before breakfast. He closes each day with a weight-lifting session motivated by the trashy teenage angst music blaring out of his headphones. His heart is set on making waves in investment banking and everyone knows he's always the safe bet for a touchdown.

You will need

Main colour: Dark
Colour two: Light
See also: You Will Need list in Yarns and Other Materials section and Abbreviations.

Body
Work as standard in *Dark*.

Head
Work as standard in *Dark* until:
Rnd 6 (Dc5, dc2 into next st) 6 times. (42)
Rnds 7–9 Dc. (3 rnds)
Rnd 10 Dc16 *Light*, dc26 *Dark*.
Rnd 11 Dc17 *Light*, dc25 *Dark*.
Rnd 12 Dc1 *Dark*, dc16 *Light*, (dc2, dc2tog) 6 times, dc1 *Dark*. (36)
Rnd 13 Dc2 *Dark*, dc15 *Light*, dc19 *Dark*.

Rnd 14 Dc2 *Dark*, dc2, dc2tog, dc4, dc2tog, dc3, dc2tog *Light*, (dc3, dc2tog) 3 times, dc4 *Dark*. (30)
Rnd 15 Dc3 *Dark*, dc10 *Light*, dc17 *Dark*.
Rnd 16 Dc3 *Dark*, (dc2tog, dc3) twice *Light*, (dc2tog, dc3) 3 times, dc2tog *Dark*. (24)
Rnd 17 Dc4 *Dark*, dc6 *Light*, dc14 *Dark*.
Rnd 18 Dc2, dc2tog in *Dark*, dc2, dc2tog, dc2 in *Light*, dc2tog, (dc2, dc2tog) 3 times in *Dark*. (18)
Rnd 19 Dc4 *Dark*, dc4 *Light*, dc10 *Dark*.
Continue to end in *Dark* only.
Rnd 20 (Dc2tog) 9 times. (9)
Rnd 21 (Dc2tog) 4 times, dc1. (5)

Ears *(make two)*
Work in *Dark*.
Rnd 1 Dc2 into next st) 6 times. (12)
Rnds 2–6 Dc. (5 rnds)
Rnd 7 (Dc2tog) 6 times. (6)

Legs *(make four)*
Work as standard in *Dark*.

Tail
Work in fur stitch every 2 sts throughout.
Working in *Dark*, ch15 and sl st to join into circle.
Rnds 1–24 Dc (with loops) in *Dark*.
Rnds 25–28 Dc (with loops) in *Light*. (4 rnds)
Rnd 29 (Dc2tog) 7 times, dc1. (8)

Making Up
See the Standard Increase and Adding Face Details sections.

Notes

Stuff the tail.
You may wish to sew the bottom of the tail up the back by a few
centimetres to ensure that it sits up behind the head.

Noah

The Zwartbles Sheep

Noah is a local vicar and borderline saint who tends to his flock more attentively than a ewe does her lambs. In his lifetime he has raised hundreds of thousands for church roofs, children's hospitals and third-world emergency aid. Whether running a marathon dressed as a chicken, having his legs waxed or climbing mountains where only goats dare go, this sheep has done it all in the name of charity. Every year he becomes a gift-giving elf at the local school Christmas fair, and has high hopes to one day swap up to the big red suit.

You will need

Main colour: Dark
Colour two: Medium
Colour three: Light (scrap)
See also: You Will Need list in Yarns and Other Materials section and Abbreviations.

Body
Work as standard in *Dark*.

Head
Work as standard in *Dark* until:
Rnd 6 (Dc5, dc2 into next st) 6 times. (42)
Rnds 7–9 Dc8 *Light*, dc34 *Dark*.
Rnd 10 Dc1 *Dark*, dc7 *Light*, dc34 *Dark*.
Rnd 11 Dc2 *Dark*, dc6 *Light*, dc34 *Dark*.

Rnd 12 Dc2 *Dark*, dc2, dc2tog, dc2 *Light*, dc4, dc2tog, (dc5, dc2tog) 4 times *Dark*. (36)
Rnds 13–14 Dc3 *Dark*, dc4 *Light*, dc29 *Dark*.
Rnd 15 Dc1, dc2tog *Dark*, dc1, dc2tog, dc1 *Light*, dc2tog, dc27 *Dark*. (33)
Rnd 16 Dc2tog *Dark*, dc2tog, dc1 *Light*, dc2tog, dc26 *Dark*. (30)
Rnd 17 Dc1 *Dark*, dc3 *Light*, dc26 *Dark*.
Rnd 18 Dc1 *Dark*, dc1, dc2tog, dc1 *Light*, (dc3, dc2tog) 5 times *Dark*. (24)
Rnd 19 Dc1 *Dark*, dc23 *Light*.
Rnds 20–21 Dc in *Light*.
Rnd 22 (Dc2, dc2tog) 6 times. (18)
Rnd 23 Dc.
Rnd 24 (Dc1, dc2tog) 6 times. (12)
Rnd 25 (Dc2tog) 6 times. (6)

Ears *(make two)*
Working in *Dark*, begin by dc6 into ring.
Rnd 1 (Dc2 into next st) 6 times. (12)
Rnds 2–5 Dc. (4 rnds)
Rnd 6 (Dc2tog) 6 times. (6)

Legs *(make four)*
Work as standard in *Dark*.

Tail
Working in *Dark*, begin by dc6 into ring.
Rnd 1 (Dc2 into next st) 6 times. (12)
Rnds 2–4 Dc. (3 rnds)
Rnd 5 (Dc2tog) 6 times. (6)
Rnd 6 Dc.

Fleece

Work ch8 loops all over the body leaving the bottom where the legs are attached plain to ensure balance when sitting.

Making Up
See the Stuffing and Sewing and Adding Face Details sections.

Notes
Sew on all parts before working the fleece.

Christophe

The Wolf

Christophe is nervously awaiting the birth of his first litter of cubs. To onlookers he appears excitedly calm, but internally he is in turmoil and utterly petrified. The more antenatal classes he attends the worse it gets, and he's too scared to read the next chapter of the new dad book he knows he should have completed by now. Despite all his anxiety over the impending life-changing event, everyone around him knows that with his fun-loving nature and big heart he will make the best father any young wolf could hope for.

You will need

Main colour: Dark
Colour two: Light
See also: You Will Need list in Yarns and Other Materials section and Abbreviations.

Body
Work as standard *Dark*.

Head
Work as standard in *Dark* until:
Rnd 6 (Dc5, dc2 into next st) 6 times. (42)
Rnds 7–8 Dc.
Rnd 9 Dc34 *Dark*, dc8 *Light*.
Rnd 10 Dc18 *Light*, dc17 *Dark*, dc7 *Light*.
Rnd 11 Dc18 *Light* dc 18 *Dark*, dc6 *Light*.

Rnd 12 Dc18 *Light*, (dc1, dc2tog) 6 times *Dark*, dc1 *Dark*, dc5 *Light*. (36)
Rnd 13 Dc18 *Light*, dc15 *Dark*, dc3 *Light*.
Rnd 14 (Dc4, dc2tog) 3 times *Light*, (dc4, dc2tog) twice, dc4 *Dark*, dc2tog *Light*. (30)
Rnd 15 Dc15 *Light*, dc15 *Dark*
Rnd 16 (Dc3, dc2tog) 3 times *Light*, (dc3, dc2tog) 3 times *Dark*. (24)
Rnd 17 Dc1 *Dark*, dc11 *Light*, dc12 *Dark*.
Rnd 18 Dc2 *Dark*, (dc2tog, dc2) twice, dc2tog *Light*, (dc2, dc2tog) 3 times *Dark*. (18)
Rnd 19 (Dc1, dc2tog) 6 times *Light*. (12)
Rnd 20 Dc *Light*.
Rnd 21 (Dc2tog) 6 times *Light*. (6)

Ears *(make two)*
Working in *Dark*, ch12 and sl st to join into circle.
Rnds 1–2 Dc.
Rnd 3 (Dc4, dc2tog) twice. (10)
Rnd 4 (Dc3, dc2tog) twice. (8)
Rnd 5 (Dc2, dc2tog) twice. (6)
Change to *Light*.
Rnd 6 (Dc1, dc2tog) twice. (4)
Rnd 7 Dc.
Rnd 8 (Dc2tog) twice. (2)

Legs *(make four)*
Work as standard in *Dark*.

Tail
Working in *Dark*, ch8 and sl st to join into circle.
Rnds 1–4 Dc.
Rnd 5 (Dc3, dc2 into next st) twice. (10)
Rnds 6–9 Dc. (4 rnds)

Rnd 10 (Dc4, dc2 into next st) twice. (12)
Rnds 11–18 Dc. (8 rnds)
Change to *Light*.
Rnd 19 (Dc5, dc2 into next st) twice. (14)
Rnds 20–22 Dc. (3 rnds)
Rnd 23 (Dc2tog) 7 times. (7)
Rnd 24 (Dc2tog) 3 times, dc1. (4)

Making Up
See the Stuffing and Sewing and Adding Face Details sections.

Notes
Stuff the end of the tail only then dc the other end flat.

TECHNICALS

In the following pages I aim to equip a complete beginner with the tools to make any or all of the menagerie animals. Even if you are a seasoned crocheter, take the time to glance over the instructions as certain techniques, such as decreasing and colour changing, may be new to you.

Basic skills

Counting

A basic skill to get yourself out of trouble is counting the number of stitches at the end of a round. After each round involving decreasing or increasing instructions, the number at the end in brackets will indicate how many stitches you should now have to work with. If you complete a round and this number is incorrect, simply pull back the round to your marker on the previous round and rework it.

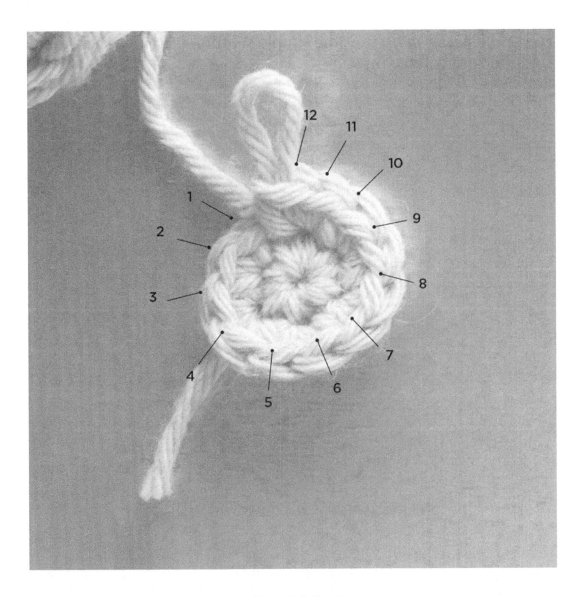

Right side and wrong side of fabric

Another essential skill is learning to recognize the right side (RS) from the wrong side (WS) of the fabric. If you are right-handed and crocheting with the RS facing outwards, you will be moving in an anti-clockwise direction (that is, from right to left) around the piece you are making, pushing the hook into the fabric from the outside to the inside. It is a very easy mistake to work an animal inside out; if you find it easier to do this, the simple solution is to turn the animal right side out before you stuff it.

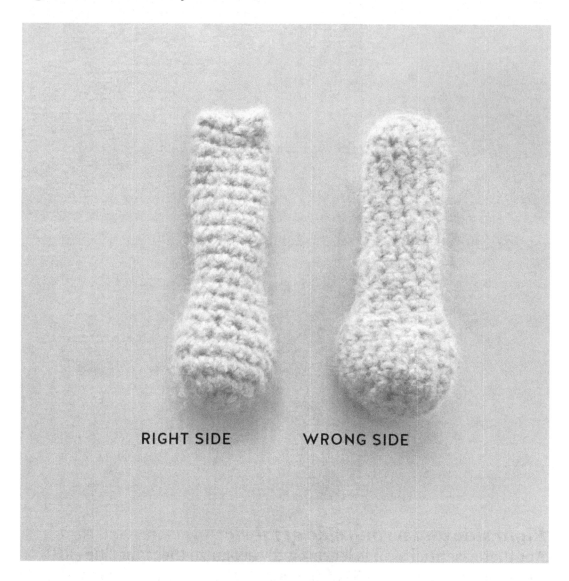

RIGHT SIDE   WRONG SIDE

Marking
Use a stitch marker to keep track of the end of each round as you work. I recommend tying in a piece of contrast yarn approximately 15cm (6in) long after the end of Rnd 2 (18 sts); as you get back

around to it, pull it forwards or backwards over your stitches to weave a marker up your fabric. The marker can be removed when finished.

160

ABBREVIATIONS

Ch: Chain. A chain is the most fundamental of all crochet stitches.

Dc: Double crochet. Using the double crochet stitch creates a compact and dense fabric. (NB: this is known as sc – single crochet – in US terminology.)

Dc2tog: Double crochet two stitches together (decrease by one stitch).

Dc3tog: Double crochet three stitches together (decrease by two stitches).

Dc4tog: Double crochet four stitches together (decrease by three stitches).

Rnd: Round. A round is a complete rotation in a spiral back to your stitch marker. With these patterns you DO NOT slip stitch at the end of a round to make a circle, but instead continue straight onto the next round in a spiral.

RS: Right side. The right side of your fabric will show small 'V' shapes in horizontal lines and will form the outside of the animal.

Sl st: Slip stitch. This is the simplest crochet stitch.

St(s): Stitch(es). You can count your stitches around the edge of your fabric.

WS: Wrong side. The wrong side of your fabric will have vertical spiralling furrows. This is where you have all the ends or strands of yarn, and it and forms the inside of the animal.

Working the stitches

Slip Knot

1. Make a loop in the yarn.
2. Pull the yarn through the loop.
3. Place your hook through the loop and tighten.

Chain

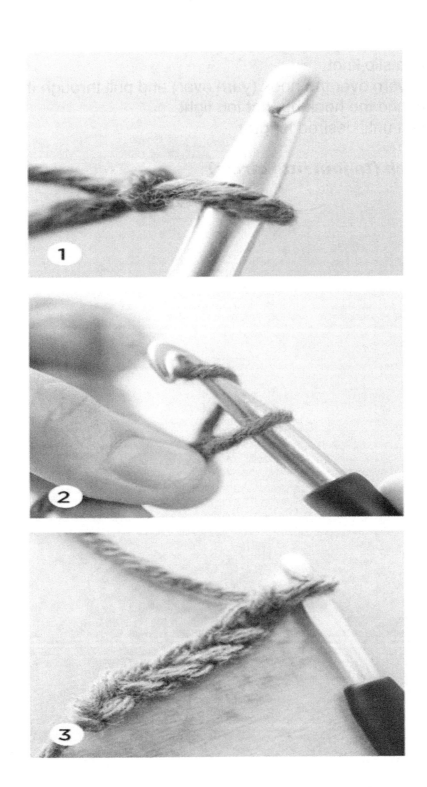

1. Make a slip knot.
2. Wrap yarn over the hook (yarn over) and pull through the loop close around the hook but not too tight.
3. Repeat until desired length.

Slip Stitch (to join into circle)

1. Insert the hook into the stitch closest to the slip knot.
2. Yarn over hook.
3. Pull the yarn through the stitch and loop in one motion.

Foundation Ring (dc6 into ring)

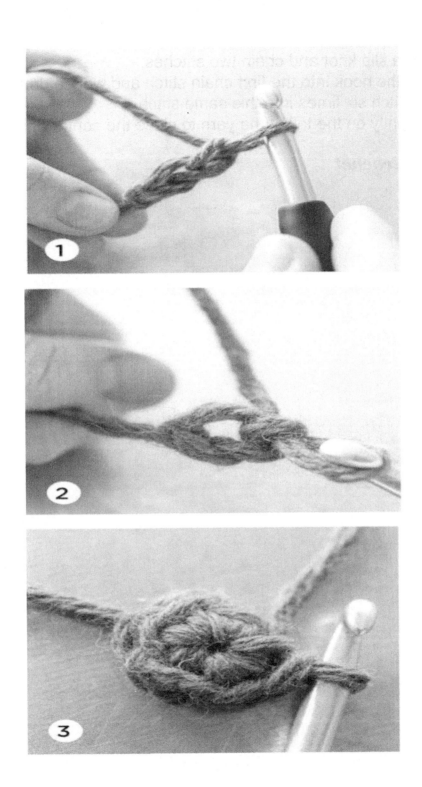

1. Make a slip knot and chain two stitches.
2. Insert the hook into the first chain stitch and work a double crochet stitch six times into this same stitch.
3. Pull tightly on the tail of the yarn to close the centre of the circle.

Double Crochet

1. Insert the hook through the stitch (both loops).
2. Yarn over and pull through the stitch.
3. Yarn over again and pull through both loops to end with one stitch.

NB: US crocheters will know this stitch as single crochet (sc).

Decrease (dc2tog)

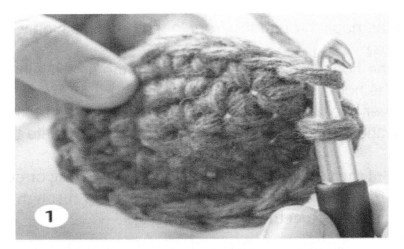

1. Insert the hook through the front loop of the stitch only (two loops on the hook).
2. Insert the hook through the front loop of the next stitch (three loops on the hook).
3. Yarn over hook and pull through first two loops on the hook, then yarn over and through both remaining loops to complete the double crochet.

NB: Some of the pattern instructions require a dc3tog or dc4tog. Work these decreases using the same method but through the stated number of stitches together.

Fur stitch

1. Wrap the yarn from front to back over the thumb of your non-hook hand.

2. Insert the hook into the stitch and yarn over with the yarn behind your thumb.

3. Pull through leaving a loop on the WS and complete the double crochet stitch with a yarn over and pull through the two loops back to one.

4. Work frequency as directed in pattern.

Colour Changes

1. Insert the hook through the next stitch, yarn over and pull through the stitch.
2. Yarn over with the new colour and complete the double crochet stitch with this new yarn.
3. Continue with this new colour, leaving the original colour to the back of the work. Cut if a one-off colour change or run on the WS of the fabric if colour changing back to it.

Slip stitch traverse

1. Make a slip knot and insert the hook into the fabric around a stitch.
2. Yarn over and pull through the fabric and loop in one motion.
3. Continue moving across the fabric like this to reach the desired location.

INSIDE OUT

When making complex colour changes that require you to run the yarn behind the fabric on the inside of the animals, make sure you don't pull the threads too tight when changing the colour as this will pucker the fabric.

Adding body details

Many of the body details are added once the main work of crocheting and assembling the toy has been done.

The most common type of tail is based on a big chain made by holding four strands of the yarn together. The tails are finished by working the number of chain loops stated in the pattern to the bottom of that big chain, which you can do with your regular hook. Lots of the animals are then completed with loops of chain stitches to represent long hair such as fleece, manes and topknots. This is worked as part of the final finishing process and should not be confused with the fur stitch, which is worked into the crocheting of the actual body part.

Chain Tails

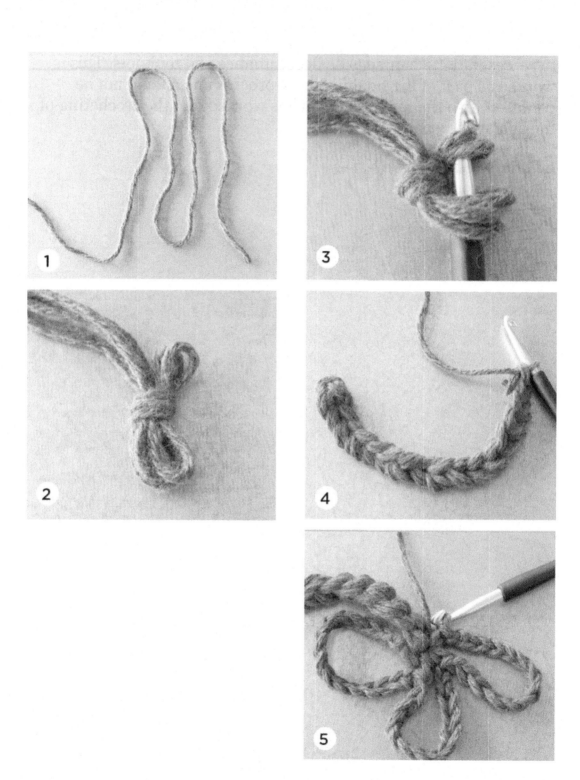

1. Fold the yarn to create a piece approximately 20cm (8in) long that is four strands thick.
2. Tie a slip knot into these four strands at one end.
3. Insert hook through both loops either side of slip knot.
4. Loosely chain the number of thick stitches stated in the pattern.
5. Into the final stitch work further chains using a single strand of yarn creating loops as stated in the pattern.

Chain Loops for Hair

1. Make a slip knot and insert the hook through the fabric at the desired position of the first loop.
2. Dc through the fabric to secure and then * chain the number of stitches stated in the pattern. Attach the chain back to the fabric with a dc approximately every other stitch and row space away from the last one.
3. Repeat from *.

Stuffing and sewing

When stuffing your animal remember that you want to show off its shape, but don't want to make it too firm and hard. Much of the appeal with this collection comes from the drape of the body, which is created through a combination of the luxury yarn and light-handed stuffing. Once you have crocheted the pieces and pushed the stuffing into them, you will need to roll and manipulate the pieces in your hands to spread the stuffing evenly and ensure the best shape.

Stuffing the bodies
All the bodies are stuffed. With the long-necked animals, be aware that you will need to make the bodies slightly firmer to ensure they hold their heads up straight.

Stuffing the heads
All the heads are stuffed at the point at which the number of stitches drops to 6, as instructed in the section on Standard Forms. The instructions for stuffing any other pieces such as horns will be detailed in the individual patterns.

Finishing the ears
The ears are not stuffed; see Adding Face Details for advice on positioning them.

Finishing the feet and legs
What gives *Edward's Menagerie* its unique appeal is the stuffing method of padding out the animals' feet but leaving their legs hollow and flat. In order for the animals to sit up on your mantlepiece,

nursery shelf or dashboard you need to splay the legs so the animals balance forwards onto their tummies.

Stuffing the tails
The instructions for stuffing the tails are detailed in the individual patterns. They are all attached in the same location on the body.

OVER STUFFED   JUST RIGHT

Order of sewing
1. Sew on the head with two stitches between the top of the body and under the head. Then oversew around these stitches in a small circle between the two parts to secure.
2. Sew the front legs to the top of the body.
3. Sew the back legs to the bottom of the body in a splayed position.
4. Sew on the ears and add any facial details.

5. Sew the tail into position.
6. Add any further details such as fleece or mane if required.

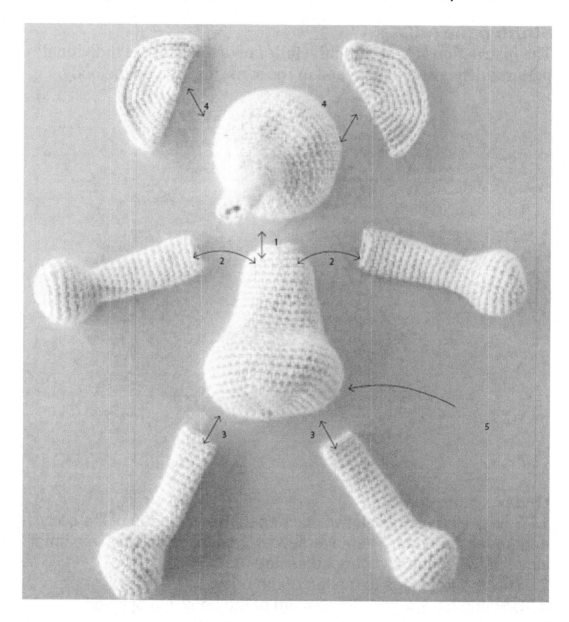

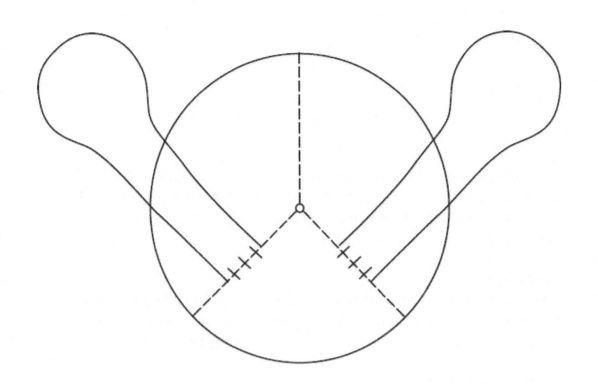

BACK LEG
POSITION

Adding face details

Sewing on the face details is when your animal's personality really begins to emerge. Take your time to get this right; don't be afraid to cut it all off and start again (I do this frequently when working on a new animal).

sewing on ears
Unless otherwise detailed in the individual pattern instructions, you will need to pinch together the bottom of an ear and sew a couple of stitches through before stitching it in place on the head.

sewing on eyes
When sewing the eyes I have used a simple method of two wraps of yarn running vertically through the same stitches across two rows. Using more wraps to create bigger eyes will make the animal look cuter and younger. Using small wraps over only one row of stitches will potentially make the animal look a bit evil! Sewing the eyes close together will give a different style than if they are set far apart. My advice would be to play with the positioning to find the way that you prefer the eyes, but in general split the face into thirds to position them.

Positioning the Ears
The position of the ears can portray the mood of the animal. Placing them to the side of the head and pointing forwards and down will give a sad and sleepy appearance. Conversely, placing them high on the top of the head will suggest that the animal is surprised or alert, so there is often a balance somewhere in between the two. The most important factor is to get the two ears evenly placed, so mark the

central stitch at the top of the head and count out from there along the same row.

SLEEPY JUST RIGHT STARTLED!

making the noses

The noses vary significantly from animal to animal. Some just have simple nostrils; others have large triangular noses with the suggestion of a mouth, and others have none at all. You could use the same overdyed black thread that you are using for the eyes, although using a lighter shade of yarn can often give the animal 'softness'; this is used to great effect in certain animals such as Emma the Bunny.

sewing on nostrils

When making nostrils, vertically oversew around one stitch. The distance you choose to separate the nostrils will help shape the character of your animal. In the case of animals with dark faces you may want to use a lighter yarn to add detail.

sewing on a triangle nose

1. Secure the yarn in the top right position for the nose.
2. Sew across three stitches horizontally from right to left and then beneath the fabric three rows down.
3. Loop the yarn over the horizontal stitch and sew back into the bottom stitch.
4. Add further wraps following a similar pattern to increase the size as desired.

WASHING

If made in natural yarn and stuffed with synthetic stuffing material, the animals can either be washed by hand or on a gentle cold machine cycle. Please be aware that if you opt to use beans, pellets or sand in your toys this may make them unwashable; you would need to sponge the surface clean.

safety

Your animal will only be as safe as you make it, so don't skimp on the stitches when sewing up. With ears and legs, I oversew all the way around the edges – you really can't sew them too much! I have also only used yarn to sew on eyes. You could use beads or buttons as an alternative. Never use toy safety eyes, beads or buttons on an animal intended for a child under three years old; you should embroider the details instead.

Topknots and tails

Don't be afraid of pinching and stitching the parts to add shape to the ear or tail as this will create expression and character, and remember to go easy on the hair loops as if you add too many your animal will become top heavy.

1. Bridget has the most universal tail type and instructions can be found in the Technicals section. Refer to this when making Georgina, Rufus, Angharad, Douglas, Alice, Audrey, Sarah and Caitlin.
2. Alexandre has a long tail worked as a hollow unstuffed tube in the same way as Juno's, Laurence's, Martin's, Siegfried's and Hamlet's.
3. Emma has a unique stuffed bob tail.
4. Austin has a simple multiple strand chain tail.
5. Richard has a short curling tail, as does Claudia.
6. Winston has a long stuffed tail that should be sewn on curving upwards.
7. Noah's short tail should be sewn on before working the fleece as with the other sheep Simon and Hank.
8. Chardonnay has a unique tail made from very long loops, but also note her mane as a reference for Timmy and Alice.
9. Timmy has a cute short stuffed tail curving upwards.
10. Esme has a touch of stuffing in her tail as does Christophe.
11. Boris has a flamboyant stuffed tail sewn into an upright position, the same as his cousin Bradlee.
12. Francis has a back covered in wonderfully textured spikes but no tail.
13. Jessie has a magnificent tail that is left unstuffed.

14. <u>Seamus</u> has a small tail that is pinched at the end and sewn pointing downwards. Use this as a reference for <u>Piotr</u>, <u>Penelope</u> and <u>Fiona</u>.

15. <u>Clarence</u> does not have a tail and shares this with <u>Germaine</u>, <u>Benedict</u>, <u>Samuel</u> and <u>Blake</u> (who needs a tail when you've got hair like that?).

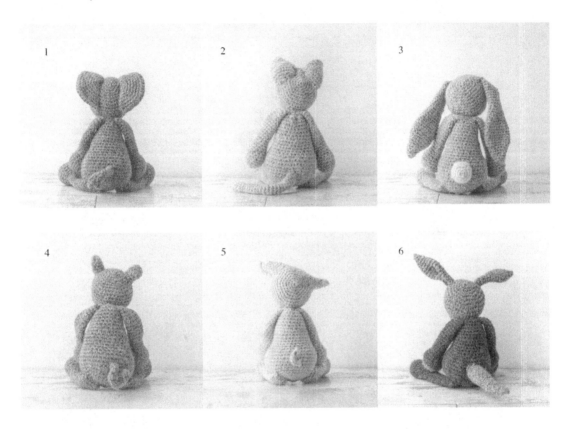

Variations

Once you have mastered the basics you can have fun with *Edward's Menagerie* to customize your own animals.

Cool Cats
Colour changing can make a significant difference to the appearance of the shape.
Alexandre is worked using only one colour.
Juno uses simple colour changing to create breed markings.
Martin uses complex colour changing to create a random pattern and is great for using up lots of short ends of yarn.
Why not try mimicking your own pet's markings?
Please share your creations with me using #edsanimals.

ALEXANDRE   JUNO   MARTIN

Counting Sheep

Noah is made using complex colour changing to add detail.
Simon is worked simply in one colour with a clean face.
Hank is made in the same way as Simon but using two colours and
with the fleece extended up onto his head.
Why not add horns or vary the fleece length?
Please share your creations with me using #edsanimals.

NOAH   SIMON   HANK

Made in the USA
Las Vegas, NV
19 February 2024

85991299R00125